Business Finance Allstars

WORKBOOK

By
Gaylen K. Bunker, MBA, CPA

www.businessallstars.com is a support web site
where calculation and assessment tools may be found.
Crossword puzzles was made with the assistance of
http://www.puzzle-maker.com/crossword_Preview.cgi

Table of Contents

Introduction

Acknowledgements

I want to express appreciation for the generous contributions made by my wife, Diane, who has read and reread the manuscript many times and given extremely valuable input. I also want to thank her for helping me to realize the importance of accounting as a fundamental tool in everyone's tool bag.

Gaylen K. Bunker

Introduction

This workbook is intended to provide students with examples of the application of the various financial models from the BFA Calculator. There are forty keys in the calculator that each accesses either a model or set of questions to help the student learn basic principles of finance. Models are either coded in HTML/Java Script (functional on most electronic devices) or designed in EXCEL and accessible wherever Microsoft is present. Usually, the first model will be shown in HTML, but if the student would prefer the EXCEL application they can click on the "XL" in the upper left hand corner and that model will appear.

The keys are divided into six different sets based on color: (1) Gray for sets of questions from readings; (2) Red for models that are foundational and support all other applications; (3) Purple for models that relate to a company's "Financing" decisions; (4) Blue for models that relate to a company's "Investing" decisions; (5) Green for models that relate to a company's "Operating" decisions; and (6) Gold for models that relate to "Valuation" of the company.

Some students feel some frustration with pre-programed models that don't allow them the opportunity to develop their own application for a better understanding of how calculations are made. It has been the experience of the author that most often when students are directed to make a spreadsheet model, they invariably make fundamental errors that lead to incorrect answers. For this reason these models were developed to provide the student with a guide to the best results. The student is invited to make their own model and test it against those provided in this workbook.

In addition, the goal of this book is to help students find real world sources of financial data, determine which elements to select, and organize data for entry into specific input cells. Then when results are generated by the models, the students will be pressed to make decisions about how to use the output. So often in the real world the critical factor is not in crunching the numbers, but where did the number come from and how do you interpret and use the results.

There are a lot of models and it can lead to some confusion about when to use each one. This workbook demonstrates each model (where applicable) by entering data for Dollar General and Family Dollar Stores as of their 2012 fiscal year ends. These companies were selected because they are both in the same industry and could be potential merger and/or acquisition candidates. After most of the models have been completed, there is a "Summary" page that allows the student to enter various results for organizational purposes. The next step is for the student to determine if one of the companies should be the target or the acquiring entity in an M&A analysis.

After most models there are exercises to help the student test the models. One of the most important things is for the student to be consistent in using the correct data. Through the use of an instructor selected company the student's answers can be compared for consistency of understanding. This is the first edition of this workbook and there may be some inadvertent errors. Any student who finds errors or mistakes in the text, applications, or calculations will be rewarded.

Gaylen K. Bunker

Lesson 1: Accounting & Generating Financial Statements

Purpose: Learn the basics of accounting transactions, how they are categorized into accounts and summarized into financial statements.

Application: Use the "ACC" tool found at www.businessallstars.com/calculator to access an excel spreadsheet that is preformatted with a grid of accounts grouped into Assets and Claims and ready for twelve unique transactions. At the bottom is a preformatted set of financial statements. The student will place the cursor over one of the line numbers to reveal a transaction and then enter it in double entry fashion in the grid.

	A	B	C	D	E	F	G	H	I	J	K	L	M	N
1				Assets							Claims			
2		Cash	A/R	Inventory	Supplies	F/A	A/D	=	A/P	N/P	LTD	C/S	R/E	Desc.
3	Bal							=						
4	1							=						
5	2							=						
6	3							=						
7	4							=						
8	5							=						
9	6							=						
10	7							=						
11	8							=						
12	9							=						
13	10							=						
14	11							=						
15	12							=						
16	Bal							=						
17	Dif							=						

Balance Sheet				Income Statement		Stmt of Cash Flow Direct Method		Stmt of Cash Flow Indirect Method	
Assets	End Bal	Beg Bal		Revenue		Cash Coll		Net Inc	
Cash				COGS		Inv Purch		Depr Exp	
Acct Rec				Gross Pft	$ -	Sup. Purch		A/R Chng	
Inventory				Oper Exp		Oper Exp.		Inv Chng	
Supplies				Depr Exp		Tax Paid		Sup Chng	
Cur Assts	$ -	$ -		EBIT	$ -	CFFO	$ -	A/P Chng	
Fix Assts				Int Exp				CFFO	$ -
Acc Depr				EBT	$ -				
Net F/A	$ -	$ -		Taxes		F/A Purch			
Total Asst	$ -	$ -		Net Inc	$ -	CFFI	$ -	F/A Purch	
Claims								CFFI	$ -
Acc Pay				Stmt of Ret Earnings		Div Paid			
Notes Pay				Beg Bal		C/S Incr		Div Paid	
Cur Liab	$ -	$ -		Net Inc	$ -	CFFF	$ -	C/S Incr	
LTDebt				Div Paid				CFFF	$ -
Tot Liab	$ -	$ -		End Bal	$ -	Cash Chng	$ -		
Com Stock						Beg Bal		Cash Chng	$ -
Ret Earn						End Bal	$ -	Beg Bal	
Com Eqty	$ -	$ -						End Bal	$ -
Tot L&OE	$ -	$ -							

Notes:_____

_____

_____

_____

Definitions
From the NYSSCPA.ORG (New York State Society of Certified Public Accountants)

Assets: An economic resource that is expected to be of benefit in the future. Probable future economic benefits obtained as a result of past transactions or events. Anything of value to which the firm has a legal claim. Any owned tangible or intangible object having economic value useful to the owner. A transaction is the act of transacting, especially a business agreement or exchange; event or condition recognized by an entry in the book account.

Cash: Asset account on a balance sheet representing paper currency and coins, negotiable money orders and checks, bank balances, and certain short-term government securities. An account is a formal record that represents, in words, money or other unit of measurement, certain resources, claims to such resources, transactions or other events that result in changes to those resources and claims.

A/R (Accounts Receivable): Claim against a debtor for an uncollected amount, generally from a completed transaction of sales or services rendered. A debtor is a party owning money or other assets to a creditor.

Inventory: Tangible property held for sale, or materials used in a production process to make a product.

Supplies:

F/A (Fixed Assets): Tangible long term assets used in the continuing operation of a business that are unlikely to change for a long time.

A/D (Accumulated Depreciation): Total depreciation pertaining to an asset or group of assets from the time the assets were placed in services until the date of the financial statement or tax return. This total is the contra account to the related asset account. Contra Account is an account considered to be an offset to another account, generally established to reduce the other account to amounts that can be realized or collected.

Claims: Liabilities and Equities representing external sources of funding and the related claim on the assets of the business until the claim is satisfied by repayment.

A/P (Accounts Payable): Amount owed to a creditor for delivered goods or completed services. A creditor is a party that loans money or other assets to another party.

N/P (Notes Payable): Collective term for written promissory notes that are due in less than one year.

LTD (Long-Term Debt): Debt with a maturity of more than one year from the current date.

C/S (Common Stock): Capital Stock having no preferences generally in terms of dividends, voting rights or distributions.

R/E (Retained Earnings): Accumulated undistributed earnings of a company retained for future needs or for future distribution to its owners.

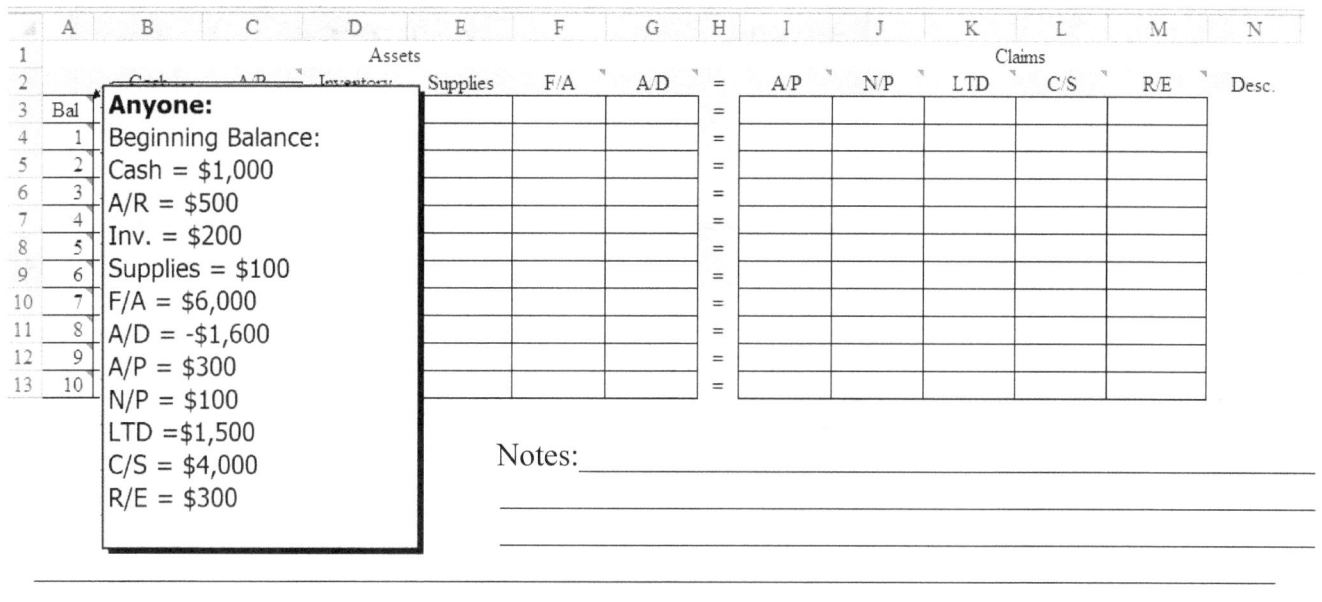

	A	B	C	D	E	F	G	H	I	J	K	L	M	N
1				Assets								Claims		
2		Cash	A/R	Inventory	Supplies	F/A	A/D	=	A/P	N/P	LTD	C/S	R/E	Desc.
3	Bal							=						
4	1							=						
5	2							=						
6	3							=						
7	4							=						
8	5							=						
9	6							=						
10	7							=						
11	8							=						
12	9							=						
13	10							=						

Notes:_____

_____

_____

_____

_____

_____

_____

	A	B	C	D	E	F	G	H	I	J	K	L	M	N
1				Assets								Claims		
2		Cash	A/R	Inventory	Supplies	F/A	A/D	=	A/P	N/P	LTD	C/S	R/E	Desc.
3	Bal	S 1,000	S 500	S 200	S 100	S 6,000	S (1,600)	=	S 300	S 100	S 1,500	S 4,000	S 300	
4	1							=						
5	2							=						

Anyone:	**Anyone:**	**Anyone:**
Owners contributed $3,000	Purchased Inventory on Account for $4,000	Recorded Sales Revenue of $6,000 on account

	A	B	C	D	E	F	G	H	I	J	K	L	M	N
1				Assets								Claims		
2		Cash	A/R	Inventory	Supplies	F/A	A/D	=	A/P	N/P	LTD	C/S	R/E	Desc.
3	Bal	S 1,000	S 500	S 200	S 100	S 6,000	S (1,600)	=	S 300	S 100	S 1,500	S 4,000	S 300	
4	1	S 3,000						=				S 3,000		
5	2			S 4,000				=	S 4,000					
6	3		S 6,000					=					S 6,000	Revenue
7	4							=						

Notes:_____

_____

_____

_____

Anyone: Recorded delivery of Inventory $3,000 related to sale in prior transaction

Anyone: Purchased Fixed Assets for cash of $2,000

Anyone: Collected $5,500 from customers for prior sales

	A	B Cash	C A/R	D Inventory	E Supplies	F F/A	G A/D	H =	I A/P	J N/P	K LTD	L C/S	M R/E	N Desc.
				Assets							Claims			
3	Bal	$ 1,000	$ 500	$ 200	$ 100	$ 6,000	$ (1,600)	=	$ 300	$ 100	$ 1,500	$ 4,000	$ 300	
4	1	$ 3,000						=				$ 3,000		
5	2			$ 4,000				=	$ 4,000					
6	3		$ 6,000					=					$ 6,000	Revenue
7	4			$ (3,000)				=					$ (3,000)	COGS
8	5	$ (2,000)				$ 2,000		=						
9	6	$ 5,500	$ (5,500)					=						
10	7							=						
11	8							–						

Notes:_____
_____
_____
_____

Anyone: Paid workers salaries of $2,000

Anyone: Recorded depreciation expense for the period of $500

Anyone: Paid $3,600 to vendors for inventory previously purchased

	A	B Cash	C A/R	D Inventory	E Supplies	F F/A	G A/D	H =	I A/P	J N/P	K LTD	L C/S	M R/E	N Desc.
				Assets							Claims			
3	Bal	$ 1,000	$ 500	$ 200	$ 100	$ 6,000	$ (1,600)	=	$ 300	$ 100	$ 1,500	$ 4,000	$ 300	
4	1	$ 3,000						=				$ 3,000		
5	2			$ 4,000				=	$ 4,000					
6	3		$ 6,000					=					$ 6,000	Revenue
7	4			$ (3,000)				=					$ (3,000)	COGS
8	5	$ (2,000)				$ 2,000		=						
9	6	$ 5,500	$ (5,500)					=						
10	7	$ (2,000)						=					$ (2,000)	S&W exp
11	8						$ (500)	=					$ (500)	Depr exp
12	9	$ (3,600)						=	$ (3,600)					
13	10							=						
14	11							–						

Notes:_____
_____
_____
_____

4

Anyone:
Paid income taxes of $200 for the period

Anyone:
Purchased supplies for cash of $50

Anyone:
Paid a dividend of $70 to investors/owners

	A	B	C	D	E	F	G	H	I	J	K	L	M	N
					Assets						Claims			
		Cash	A/R	Inventory	Supplies	F/A	A/D	=	A/P	N/P	LTD	C/S	R/E	Desc.
3	Bal	$ 1,000	$ 500	$ 200	$ 100	$ 6,000	$ (1,600)	=	$ 300	$ 100	$ 1,500	$ 4,000	$ 300	
4	1	$ 3,000						=				$ 3,000		
5	2			$ 4,000				=	$ 4,000					
6	3		$ 6,000					=					$ 6,000	Revenue
7	4			$ (3,000)				=					$ (3,000)	COGS
8	5	$ (2,000)				$ 2,000		=						
9	6	$ 5,500	$ (5,500)					=						
10	7	$ (2,000)						=					$ (2,000)	S&W exp
11	8						$ (500)	=					$ (500)	Depr exp
12	9	$ (3,600)						=	$ (3,600)					
13	10	$ (200)						=					$ (200)	Tax exp
14	11	$ (50)			$ 50			=						
15	12	$ (70)						=					$ (70)	Div Paid
16	Bal							=						
17	Dif							=						

Notes:_____

_____

_____

_____

Anyone:
Calculated Ending balances for each account

	Cash	A/R	Inventory	Supplies	F/A	A/D	=	A/P	N/P	LTD	C/S	R/E	Desc.
			Assets				=			Claims			
Bal	$ 1,000	$ 500	$ 200	$ 100	$ 6,000	$ (1,600)	=	$ 300	$ 100	$ 1,500	$ 4,000	$ 300	
1	$ 3,000						=				$ 3,000		
2			$ 4,000				=	$ 4,000					
3		$ 6,000					=					$ 6,000	Revenue
4			$ (3,000)				=					$ (3,000)	COGS
5	$ (2,000)				$ 2,000		=						
6	$ 5,500	$ (5,500)					=						
7	$ (2,000)						=					$ (2,000)	S&W exp
8						$ (500)	=					$ (500)	Depr exp
9	$ (3,600)						=	$ (3,600)					
10	$ (200)						=					$ (200)	Tax exp
11	$ (50)			$ 50			=						
12	$ (70)						=					$ (70)	Div Paid
Bal	$ 1,580	$ 1,000	$ 1,200	$ 150	$ 8,000	$ (2,100)	=	$ 700	$ 100	$ 1,500	$ 7,000	530	
Dif							=						

Notes:_____

_____

_____

_____

	A	B	C	D	E	F	G	H	I	J	K	L	M	N
1				Assets							Claims			
2		Cash	A/R	Inventory	Supplies	F/A	A/D	=	A/P	N/P	LTD	C/S	R/E	Desc.
3	Bal	$ 1,000	$ 500	$ 200	$ 100	$ 6,000	$ (1,600)	=	$ 300	$ 100	$ 1,500	$ 4,000	$ 300	
4	1	$ 3,000						=				$ 3,000		
5	2			$ 4,000				=	$ 4,000					
6	3		$ 6,000					=					$ 6,000	Revenue
7	4			$ (3,000)				=					$ (3,000)	COGS
8	5	$ (2,000)				$ 2,000		=						
9	6	$ 5,500	$ (5,500)					=						
10	7	$ (2,000)						=					$ (2,000)	S&W exp
11	8						$ (500)	=					$ (500)	Depr exp
12	9	$ (3,600)						=	$ (3,600)					
13	10	$ (200)						=					$ (200)	Tax exp
14	11	$ (50)			$ 50			=						
15	12	$ (70)						=					$ (70)	Div Paid
16	Bal	$ 1,580	$ 1,000	$ 1,200	$ 150	$ 8,000	$ (2,100)	=	$ 700	$ 100	$ 1,500	$ 7,000	530	
17	Dif							=						

Balance Sheet				Income Statement		Stmt of Cash Flow Direct Method		Stmt of Cash Flow Indirect Method	
Assets	End Bal	Beg Bal		Revenue		Cash Coll		Net Inc	
Cash		$ 1,000		COGS		Inv Purch		Depr Exp	
Acct Rec		$ 500		Gross Pft	$ -	Sup. Purch		A/R Chng	
Inventory		$ 200		Oper Exp		Oper Exp.		Inv Chng	
Supplies		$ 100		Depr Exp		Tax Paid		Sup Chng	
Cur Assts	$ -	$ 1,800		EBIT	$ -	CFFO	$ -	A/P Chng	
Fix Assts		$ 6,000		Int Exp				CFFO	$ -
Acc Depr		$ (1,600)		EBT	$ -	F/A Purch			
Net F/A	$ -	$ 4,400		Taxes		CFFI	$ -	F/A Purch	
Total Asst	$ -	$ 6,200		Net Inc	$ -			CFFI	$ -
Claims						Div Paid			
Acc Pay		$ 300		Stmt of Ret Earnings		C/S Incr		Div Paid	
Notes Pay		$ 100		Beg Bal		CFFF	$ -	C/S Incr	
Cur Liab	$ -	$ 400		Net Inc	$ -			CFFF	$ -
LTDebt		$ 1,500		Div Paid		Cash Chng	$ -		
Tot Liab	$ -	$ 1,900		End Bal	$ -	Beg Bal		Cash Chng	$ -
Com Stock		$ 4,000				End Bal	$ -	Beg Bal	
Ret Earn		$ 300						End Bal	$ -
Com Eqty	$ -	$ 4,300							
Tot L&OE	$ -	$ 6,200							

Notes:_____
_____
_____
_____

	Cash	A/R	Inventory	Supplies	F/A	A/D	=	A/P	N/P	LTD	C/S	R/E	Desc.
			Assets							Claims			
Bal	$ 1,000	$ 500	$ 200	$ 100	$ 6,000	$ (1,600)	=	$ 300	$ 100	$ 1,500	$ 4,000	$ 300	
1	$ 3,000						=				$ 3,000		
2			$ 4,000				=	$ 4,000					
3		$ 6,000					=					$ 6,000	Revenue
4			$ (3,000)				=					$ (3,000)	COGS
5	$ (2,000)				$ 2,000		=						
6	$ 5,500	$ (5,500)					=						
7	$ (2,000)						=					$ (2,000)	S&W exp
8						$ (500)	=					$ (500)	Depr exp
9	$ (3,600)						=	$ (3,600)					
10	$ (200)						=					$ (200)	Tax exp
11	$ (50)			$ 50			=						
12	$ (70)						=					$ (70)	Div Paid
Bal	$ 1,580	$ 1,000	$ 1,200	$ 150	$ 8,000	$ (2,100)	=	$ 700	$ 100	$ 1,500	$ 7,000	$ 530	
Dif							=						

Balance Sheet

Assets	End Bal	Beg Bal
Cash	$ 1,580	$ 1,000
Acct Rec	$ 1,000	$ 500
Inventory	$ 1,200	$ 200
Supplies	$ 150	$ 100
Cur Assts	$ 3,930	$ 1,800
Fix Assts	$ 8,000	$ 6,000
Acc Depr	$ (2,100)	$ (1,600)
Net F/A	$ 5,900	$ 4,400
Total Asst	$ 9,830	$ 6,200
Claims		
Acc Pay	$ 700	$ 300
Notes Pay	$ 100	$ 100
Cur Liab	$ 800	$ 400
LTDebt	$ 1,500	$ 1,500
Tot Liab	$ 2,300	$ 1,900
Com Stock	$ 7,000	$ 4,000
Ret Earn	$ 530	$ 300
Com Eqty	$ 7,530	$ 4,300
Tot L&OE	$ 9,830	$ 6,200

Income Statement

Revenue	
COGS	___
Gross Pft	$ -
Oper Exp	
Depr Exp	
EBIT	$ -
Int Exp	
EBT	$ -
Taxes	
Net Inc	$ -

Stmt of Ret Earnings

Beg Bal	
Net Inc	$ -
Div Paid	
End Bal	$ -

Stmt of Cash Flow Direct Method

Cash Coll	
Inv Purch	
Sup. Purch	
Oper Exp.	
Tax Paid	
CFFO	$ -
F/A Purch	
CFFI	$ -
Div Paid	
C/S Incr	
CFFF	$ -
Cash Chng	$ -
Beg Bal	
End Bal	$ -

Stmt of Cash Flow Indirect Method

Net Inc	
Depr Exp	
A/R Chng	
Inv Chng	
Sup Chng	
A/P Chng	
CFFO	$ -
F/A Purch	
CFFI	$ -
Div Paid	
C/S Incr	
CFFF	$ -
Cash Chng	$ -
Beg Bal	
End Bal	$ -

Notes:_____

_____

_____

_____

	A	B Cash	C A/R	D Inventory	E Supplies	F F/A	G A/D	H =	I A/P	J N/P	K LTD	L C/S	M R/E	N Desc.
1					Assets							Claims		
2		Cash	A/R	Inventory	Supplies	F/A	A/D	=	A/P	N/P	LTD	C/S	R/E	Desc.
3	Bal	$ 1,000	$ 500	$ 200	$ 100	$ 6,000	$ (1,600)	=	$ 300	$ 100	$ 1,500	$ 4,000	$ 300	
4	1	$ 3,000						=				$ 3,000		
5	2			$ 4,000				=	$ 4,000					
6	3		$ 6,000					=					$ 6,000	Revenue
7	4			$ (3,000)				=					$ (3,000)	COGS
8	5	$ (2,000)				$ 2,000		=						
9	6	$ 5,500	$ (5,500)					=						
10	7	$ (2,000)						=					$ (2,000)	S&W exp
11	8						$ (500)	=					$ (500)	Depr exp
12	9	$ (3,600)						=	$ (3,600)					
13	10	$ (200)						=					$ (200)	Tax exp
14	11	$ (50)			$ 50			=						
15	12	$ (70)						=					$ (70)	Div Paid
16	Bal	$ 1,580	$ 1,000	$ 1,200	$ 150	$ 8,000	$ (2,100)	=	$ 700	$ 100	$ 1,500	$ 7,000	$ 530	
17	Dif							=						

Balance Sheet				Income Statement			Stmt of Cash Flow Direct Method			Stmt of Cash Flow Indirect Method	
Assets	End Bal	Beg Bal		Revenue	$ 6,000		Cash Coll			Net Inc	
Cash	$ 1,580	$ 1,000		COGS	$ (3,000)		Inv Purch			Depr Exp	
Acct Rec	$ 1,000	$ 500		Gross Pft	$ 3,000		Sup. Purch			A/R Chng	
Inventory	$ 1,200	$ 200		Oper Exp	$ (2,000)		Oper Exp.			Inv Chng	
Supplies	$ 150	$ 100		Depr Exp	$ (500)		Tax Paid			Sup Chng	
Cur Assts	$ 3,930	$ 1,800		EBIT	$ 500		CFFO	$ -		A/P Chng	
Fix Assts	$ 8,000	$ 6,000		Int Exp	$ -					CFFO	$ -
Acc Depr	$ (2,100)	$ (1,600)		EBT	$ 500		F/A Purch				
Net F/A	$ 5,900	$ 4,400		Taxes	$ (200)		CFFI	$ -		F/A Purch	
Total Asst	$ 9,830	$ 6,200		Net Inc	$ 300					CFFI	$ -
Claims							Div Paid				
Acc Pay	$ 700	$ 300		Stmt of Ret Earnings			C/S Incr			Div Paid	
Notes Pay	$ 100	$ 100		Beg Bal	$ 300		CFFF	$ -		C/S Incr	
Cur Liab	$ 800	$ 400		Net Inc	$ 300					CFFF	$ -
LTDebt	$ 1,500	$ 1,500		Div Paid	$ (70)		Cash Chng	$ -			
Tot Liab	$ 2,300	$ 1,900		End Bal	$ 530		Beg Bal			Cash Chng	$ -
Com Stock	$ 7,000	$ 4,000					End Bal	$ -		Beg Bal	
Ret Earn	$ 530	$ 300								End Bal	$ -
Com Eqty	$ 7,530	$ 4,300									
Tot L&OE	$ 9,830	$ 6,200									

Notes:
_____
_____
_____
_____

9

	A	B	C	D	E	F	G	H	I	J	K	L	M	N
1						Assets						Claims		
2		Cash	A/R	Inventory	Supplies	F/A	A/D	=	A/P	N/P	LTD	C/S	R/E	Desc.
3	Bal	$ 1,000	$ 500	$ 200	$ 100	$ 6,000	$ (1,600)	=	$ 300	$ 100	$ 1,500	$ 4,000	$ 300	
4	1	$ 3,000						=				$ 3,000		
5	2			$ 4,000				=	$ 4,000					
6	3		$ 6,000					=					$ 6,000	Revenue
7	4			$ (3,000)				=					$ (3,000)	COGS
8	5	$ (2,000)				$ 2,000		=						
9	6	$ 5,500	$ (5,500)					=						
10	7	$ (2,000)						=					$ (2,000)	S&W exp
11	8						$ (500)	=					$ (500)	Depr exp
12	9	$ (3,600)						=	$ (3,600)					
13	10	$ (200)						=					$ (200)	Tax exp
14	11	$ (50)			$ 50			=						
15	12	$ (70)						=					$ (70)	Div Paid
16	Bal	$ 1,580	$ 1,000	$ 1,200	$ 150	$ 8,000	$ (2,100)	=	$ 700	$ 100	$ 1,500	$ 7,000	$ 530	
17	Dif							=						

Balance Sheet	End Bal	Beg Bal		Income Statement			Stmt of Cash Flow Direct Method			Stmt of Cash Flow Indirect Method	
Assets				Revenue	$ 6,000		Cash Coll	$ 5,500		Net Inc	
Cash	$ 1,580	$ 1,000		COGS	$ (3,000)		Inv Purch	$ (3,600)		Depr Exp	
Acct Rec	$ 1,000	$ 500		Gross Pft	$ 3,000		Sup. Purc	$ (50)		A/R Chng	
Inventory	$ 1,200	$ 200		Oper Exp	$ (2,000)		Oper Exp.	$ (2,000)		Inv Chng	
Supplies	$ 150	$ 100		Depr Exp	$ (500)		Tax Paid	$ (200)		Sup Chng	
Cur Assts	$ 3,930	$ 1,800		EBIT	$ 500		CFFO	$ (350)		A/P Chng	
Fix Assts	$ 8,000	$ 6,000		Int Exp	$ -					CFFO	$ -
Acc Depr	$ (2,100)	$ (1,600)		EBT	$ 500		F/A Purch	$ (2,000)			
Net F/A	$ 5,900	$ 4,400		Taxes	$ (200)		CFFI	$ (2,000)		F/A Purch	
Total Asst	$ 9,830	$ 6,200		Net Inc	$ 300					CFFI	$ -
Claims							Div Paid	$ (70)			
Acc Pay	$ 700	$ 300		Stmt of Ret Earnings			C/S Incr	$ 3,000		Div Paid	
Notes Pay	$ 100	$ 100		Beg Bal	$ 300		CFFF	$ 2,930		C/S Incr	
Cur Liab	$ 800	$ 400		Net Inc	$ 300					CFFF	$ -
LTDebt	$ 1,500	$ 1,500		Div Paid	$ (70)						
Tot Liab	$ 2,300	$ 1,900		End Bal	$ 530		Cash Chng	$ 580			
Com Stock	$ 7,000	$ 4,000					Beg Bal	$ 1,000		Cash Chng	$ -
Ret Earn	$ 530	$ 300					End Bal	$ 1,580		Beg Bal	
Com Eqty	$ 7,530	$ 4,300								End Bal	$ -
Tot L&OE	$ 9,830	$ 6,200									

Notes:_____

_____

_____

_____

10

	Cash	A/R	Inventory	Supplies	F/A	A/D	=	A/P	N/P	LTD	C/S	R/E	Desc.
					Assets					Claims			
Bal	$ 1,000	$ 500	$ 200	$ 100	$ 6,000	$ (1,600)	=	$ 300	$ 100	$ 1,500	$ 4,000	$ 300	
1	$ 3,000						=				$ 3,000		
2			$ 4,000				=	$ 4,000					
3		$ 6,000					=					$ 6,000	Revenue
4			$ (3,000)				=					$ (3,000)	COGS
5	$ (2,000)				$ 2,000		=						
6	$ 5,500	$ (5,500)					=						
7	$ (2,000)						=					$ (2,000)	S&W exp
8						$ (500)	=					$ (500)	Depr exp
9	$ (3,600)						=	$ (3,600)					
10	$ (200)						=					$ (200)	Tax exp
11	$ (50)			$ 50			=						
12	$ (70)						=					$ (70)	Div Paid
Bal	$ 1,580	$ 1,000	$ 1,200	$ 150	$ 8,000	$ (2,100)	=	$ 700	$ 100	$ 1,500	$ 7,000	$ 530	
Dif							=						

(Comment box: "Anyone: Calculated the change in each account: Beg. Bal. minus End. Bal.")

Assets	End Bal	Beg Bal
Cash	$ 1,580	$ 1,000
Acct Rec	$ 1,000	$ 500
Inventory	$ 1,200	$ 200
Supplies	$ 150	$ 100
Cur Assts	$ 3,930	$ 1,800
Fix Assts	$ 8,000	$ 6,000
Acc Depr	$ (2,100)	$ (1,600)
Net F/A	$ 5,900	$ 4,400
Total Asst	$ 9,830	$ 6,200
Claims		
Acc Pay	$ 700	$ 300
Notes Pay	$ 100	$ 100
Cur Liab	$ 800	$ 400
LTDebt	$ 1,500	$ 1,500
Tot Liab	$ 2,300	$ 1,900
Com Stock	$ 7,000	$ 4,000
Ret Earn	$ 530	$ 300
Com Eqty	$ 7,530	$ 4,300
Tot L&OE	$ 9,830	$ 6,200

Income Statement

Revenue	$ 6,000
COGS	$ (3,000)
Gross Pft	$ 3,000
Oper Exp	$ (2,000)
Depr Exp	$ (500)
EBIT	$ 500
Int Exp	$ -
EBT	$ 500
Taxes	$ (200)
Net Inc	$ 300

Stmt of Ret Earnings

Beg Bal	$ 300
Net Inc	$ 300
Div Paid	$ (70)
End Bal	$ 530

Stmt of Cash Flow Direct Method

Cash Coll	$ 5,500
Inv Purch	$ (3,600)
Sup. Purc	$ (50)
Oper Exp.	$ (2,000)
Tax Paid	$ (200)
CFFO	$ (350)
F/A Purch	$ (2,000)
CFFI	$ (2,000)
Div Paid	$ (70)
C/S Incr	$ 3,000
CFFF	$ 2,930
Cash Chng	$ 580
Beg Bal	$ 1,000
End Bal	$ 1,580

Stmt of Cash Flow Indirect Method

Net Inc	
Depr Exp	
A/R Chng	
Inv Chng	
Sup Chng	
A/P Chng	
CFFO	$ -
F/A Purch	
CFFI	$ -
Div Paid	
C/S Incr	
CFFF	$ -
Cash Chng	$ -
Beg Bal	
End Bal	$ -

Notes:_____
_____
_____
_____

11

	A	B	C	D	E	F	G	H	I	J	K	L	M	N
1				Assets								Claims		
2		Cash	A/R	Inventory	Supplies	F/A	A/D	=	A/P	N/P	LTD	C/S	R/E	Desc.
3	Bal	$ 1,000	$ 500	$ 200	$ 100	$ 6,000	$ (1,600)	=	$ 300	$ 100	$ 1,500	$ 4,000	$ 300	
4	1	$ 3,000						=				$ 3,000		
5	2			$ 4,000				=	$ 4,000					
6	3		$ 6,000					=					$ 6,000	Revenue
7	4			$ (3,000)				=					$ (3,000)	COGS
8	5	$ (2,000)				$ 2,000		=						
9	6	$ 5,500	$ (5,500)					=						
10	7	$ (2,000)						=					$ (2,000)	S&W exp
11	8						$ (500)	=					$ (500)	Depr exp
12	9	$ (3,600)						=	$ (3,600)					
13	10	$ (200)						=					$ (200)	Tax exp
14	11	$ (50)			$ 50			=						
15	12	$ (70)						=					$ (70)	Div Paid
16	Bal	$ 1,580	$ 1,000	$ 1,200	$ 150	$ 8,000	$ (2,100)	=	$ 700	$ 100	$ 1,500	$ 7,000	$ 530	
17	Dif	$ 580	$ 500	$ 1,000	$ 50	$ 2,000	$ (500)	=	$ 400	$ -	$ -	$ 3,000	$ 230	

Balance Sheet	End Bal	Beg Bal		Income Statement			Stmt of Cash Flow Direct Method			Stmt of Cash Flow Indirect Method	
Assets	End Bal	Beg Bal		Revenue	$ 6,000					Net Inc	
Cash	$ 1,580	$ 1,000		COGS	$ (3,000)		Cash Coll	$ 5,500		Depr Exp	
Acct Rec	$ 1,000	$ 500		Gross Pft	$ 3,000		Inv Purch	$ (3,600)		A/R Chng	
Inventory	$ 1,200	$ 200		Oper Exp	$ (2,000)		Sup. Purc	$ (50)		Inv Chng	
Supplies	$ 150	$ 100		Depr Exp	$ (500)		Oper Exp.	$ (2,000)		Sup Chng	
Cur Assts	$ 3,930	$ 1,800		EBIT	$ 500		Tax Paid	$ (200)		A/P Chng	
Fix Assts	$ 8,000	$ 6,000		Int Exp	$ -		CFFO	$ (350)		CFFO	$ -
Acc Depr	$ (2,100)	$ (1,600)		EBT	$ 500						
Net F/A	$ 5,900	$ 4,400		Taxes	$ (200)		F/A Purch	$ (2,000)		F/A Purch	
Total Asst	$ 9,830	$ 6,200		Net Inc	$ 300		CFFI	$ (2,000)		CFFI	$ -
Claims											
Acc Pay	$ 700	$ 300		Stmt of Ret Earnings			Div Paid	$ (70)			
Notes Pay	$ 100	$ 100		Beg Bal	$ 300		C/S Incr	$ 3,000		Div Paid	
Cur Liab	$ 800	$ 400		Net Inc	$ 300		CFFF	$ 2,930		C/S Incr	
LTDebt	$ 1,500	$ 1,500		Div Paid	$ (70)					CFFF	$ -
Tot Liab	$ 2,300	$ 1,900		End Bal	$ 530		Cash Chng	$ 580			
Com Stock	$ 7,000	$ 4,000					Beg Bal	$ 1,000		Cash Chng	$ -
Ret Earn	$ 530	$ 300					End Bal	$ 1,580		Beg Bal	
Com Eqty	$ 7,530	$ 4,300								End Bal	$ -
Tot L&OE	$ 9,830	$ 6,200									

Notes:_____

_____

_____

_____

12

	Cash	A/R	Inventory	Supplies	F/A	A/D	=	A/P	N/P	LTD	C/S	R/E	Desc.
			Assets				=			Claims			
Bal	$ 1,000	$ 500	$ 200	$ 100	$ 6,000	$ (1,600)	=	$ 300	$ 100	$ 1,500	$ 4,000	$ 300	
1	$ 3,000						=				$ 3,000		
2			$ 4,000				=	$ 4,000					
3		$ 6,000					=					$ 6,000	Revenue
4			$ (3,000)				=					$ (3,000)	COGS
5	$ (2,000)				$ 2,000		=						
6	$ 5,500	$ (5,500)					=						
7	$ (2,000)						=					$ (2,000)	S&W exp
8						$ (500)	=					$ (500)	Depr exp
9	$ (3,600)						=	$ (3,600)					
10	$ (200)						=					$ (200)	Tax exp
11	$ (50)			$ 50			=						
12	$ (70)						=					$ (70)	Div Paid
Bal	$ 1,580	$ 1,000	$ 1,200	$ 150	$ 8,000	$ (2,100)	=	$ 700	$ 100	$ 1,500	$ 7,000	$ 530	
Dif	$ 580	$ 500	$ 1,000	$ 50	$ 2,000	$ (500)	=	$ 400	$ -	$ -	$ 3,000	$ 230	

Balance Sheet

Assets	End Bal	Beg Bal
Cash	$ 1,580	$ 1,000
Acct Rec	$ 1,000	$ 500
Inventory	$ 1,200	$ 200
Supplies	$ 150	$ 100
Cur Assts	$ 3,930	$ 1,800
Fix Assts	$ 8,000	$ 6,000
Acc Depr	$ (2,100)	$ (1,600)
Net F/A	$ 5,900	$ 4,400
Total Asst	$ 9,830	$ 6,200
Claims		
Acc Pay	$ 700	$ 300
Notes Pay	$ 100	$ 100
Cur Liab	$ 800	$ 400
LTDebt	$ 1,500	$ 1,500
Tot Liab	$ 2,300	$ 1,900
Com Stock	$ 7,000	$ 4,000
Ret Earn	$ 530	$ 300
Com Eqty	$ 7,530	$ 4,300
Tot L&OE	$ 9,830	$ 6,200

Income Statement

Revenue	$ 6,000
COGS	$ (3,000)
Gross Pft	$ 3,000
Oper Exp	$ (2,000)
Depr Exp	$ (500)
EBIT	$ 500
Int Exp	$ -
EBT	$ 500
Taxes	$ (200)
Net Inc	$ 300

Stmt of Ret Earnings

Beg Bal	$ 300
Net Inc	$ 300
Div Paid	$ (70)
End Bal	$ 530

Stmt of Cash Flow Direct Method

Cash Coll	$ 5,500
Inv Purch	$ (3,600)
Sup. Purc	$ (50)
Oper Exp.	$ (2,000)
Tax Paid	$ (200)
CFFO	$ (350)
F/A Purch	$ (2,000)
CFFI	$ (2,000)
Div Paid	$ (70)
C/S Incr	$ 3,000
CFFF	$ 2,930
Cash Chng	$ 580
Beg Bal	$ 1,000
End Bal	$ 1,580

Stmt of Cash Flow Indirect Method

Net Inc	$ 300
Depr Exp	$ 500
A/R Chng	$ (500)
Inv Chng	$ (1,000)
Sup Chng	$ (50)
A/P Chng	$ 400
CFFO	$ (350)
F/A Purch	$ (2,000)
CFFI	$ (2,000)
Div Paid	$ (70)
C/S Incr	$ 3,000
CFFF	$ 2,930
Cash Chng	$ 580
Beg Bal	$ 1,000
End Bal	$ 1,580

Notes:_____

_____

_____

_____

13

Lesson 1 Exercises

1-1.

		Fill each Box with a single Letter representing an Answer from the list at right	Answers
1.		Fixed Assets	A. Asset
2.		Long-Term Debt	C. Claim
3.		Cash	
4.		Notes Payable	
5.		Accumulated Depreciation	
6.		Other Assets	
7.		Marketable Securities	
8.		Accounts Receivable	
9.		Accounts Payable	
10.		Commons Stock	
11.		Taxes Payable	
12.		Supplies	
13.		Retained Earnings	
14.		Inventory	
15.		Accrued Liabilities	

1-2.

		Fill each Box with a single Letter representing an Answer from the list at right	Answers
1.		Interest Expense	I. Income Statement
2.		Long-Term Debt	B. Balance Sheet
3.		Cash	
4.		Notes Payable	
5.		Depreciation Expense	
6.		Net Income	
7.		Marketable Securities	
8.		Accounts Receivable	
9.		Revenue	
10.		Cost of Goods Sold	
11.		Taxes Payable	
12.		Supplies	
13.		Retained Earnings	
14.		Inventory	
15.		Salary & Wage Expense	

1-3.

	Fill each Box with a single Letter representing an Answer from the list at right	Answers
1.	Cash Collections	I. Indirect Method
2.	Change in Accounts Receivable	D. Direct Method
3.	Cash Flows from Operations	B. Both of them
4.	Fixed Asset Spending	
5.	Inventory Purchases	
6.	Operating Expenses paid	
7.	Dividends Paid	
8.	Change in Accounts Payable	
9.	Depreciation Expense	
10.	Change in Inventory	
11.	Supplies Purchases	
12.	Change in Supplies	
13.	Common Stock Issued	
14.	Income Taxes Paid	
15.	Net Income	

1-4.

#	Cash	A/R	Inven	Sup	F/A	A/D	=	A/P	N/P	LTD	C/S	R/E	Desc
0	1000	500	200	100	6000	-1600	=	300	100	1500	4000	300	Beg Bal
1							=						
2							=						
3							=						
4							=						
5							=						
6							=						
7							=						
8							=						
9							=						
10							=						

Enter amounts for each numbered transaction below in the correct line number and accounts above

1. Acquired $500 worth of inventory on account.

2. Purchased $100 worth of supplies with cash.

3. Borrowed $1000 from the bank on a short-term note.

4. Recorded sales to customers worth $1500 on account.

5. Delivered the inventory to customers that cost $800.

6. Collected $500 from prior sales to customers.

7. Paid $300 Salaries and Wages for the period.

8. Recorded $200 of depreciation for the period.

9. Paid vendors $300 for prior purchases.

10. Paid income taxes of $200.

1-5

#	Cash	A/R	Inven	Sup	F/A	A/D	=	A/P	N/P	LTD	C/S	R/E	Desc
0	1000	500	200	100	6000	-1600	=	300	100	1500	4000	300	Beg Bal
1							=						
2							=						
3							=						
4							=						
5							=						
6							=						
7							=						
8							=						
9							=						
10							=						

Enter amounts for each numbered transaction below in the correct line number and accounts above

1. Acquired $2000 worth of inventory on account.

2. Borrowed $3000 from the bank on a short-term note.

3. Received $1000 from customers for current sales.

4. Delivered $500 worth of inventory to customers

5. Sold customers $800 of inventory on account.

6. Delivered $400 worth of inventory to customers.

7. Purchased $500 worth of inventory for cash.

8. Paid $500 to vendors for prior purchases of inventory.

9. Obsolete inventory valued at $200 was writen-off.

10. Determined that $200 of prior customers sales were uncollectible and a bad debt expense.

1-6.

#	Cash	M/S	A/R	Sup	F/A	A/D	=	A/P	T/P	LTD	C/S	R/E	Desc
0	1000	500	200	100	6000	-1600	=	300	100	1500	4000	300	Beg Bal
1							=						
2							=						
3							=						
4							=						
5							=						
6							=						
7							=						
8							=						
9							=						
10							=						

Enter amounts for each numbered transaction below in the correct line number and accounts above

1. Repaid $500 of the Long-term debt.

2. Paid $50 interest expense on the debt.

3. Wrote-off $100 as Bad Debt Expense for uncollectible accounts receivable.

4. Purchased $5000 of equipment on a long-term contract.

5. Received $200 for the sale of old equipment that had cost $1000. Wrote-off $600 of related accumulated depreciation and recognized a loss on the sale. (4 entries required)

6. Received $2000 from customers for services performed.

7. Paid rent expense of $200.

8. Paid salaries and wages of $1000.

9. Recorded Income Tax Expense of $300 that was owed, but not yet paid.

10. Transferred $100 from cash into marketable securities for short-term investment.

1-7.

#	Cash	A/R	Inv	Sup	F/A	A/D	=	A/P	N/P	LTD	C/S	R/E	Desc
1	500	1000	400	100	4000	-1500	=	600	800	2000	1000	100	Beg. Bal.
2	5000						=			5000			
3			2000				=	2000					
4		3000					=					3000	Revenue
5			-1800				=					-1800	COGS
6	-600						=					-600	Oper. Exp.
7	-1000						=	-1000					
8	2000	-2000					=						
9				-50			=					-50	Sup. Exp.
10					2000		=			2000			
11						-250	=					-250	Depr. Exp.
12	-120						=					-120	Tax Exp.
13	1000						=				1000		
14	-80						=					-80	Dividend
15	6700	2000	600	50	6000	-1750	=	1600	800	9000	2000	200	End. Bal.
16	6200	1000	200	-50	2000	-250		1000	0	7000	1000	100	Change

Enter the answer to each question below based on the data above.

1.		What is the Gross Profit?
2.		What is the Net Income?
3.		What is the beginning balance of Total Assets?
4.		What is the ending balance of Total Assets?
5.		What is the beginning balance of Net Fixed Assets?
6.		What is the ending balance of Net Fixed Assets?
7.		What is the beginning Current Assets total?
8.		What is the ending Current Liabilities total (include N/P)?
9.		What is the Operating Cash Flow?
10.		What is the Investing Cash Flow?
11.		What is the Financing Cash Flow?
12.		What is the beginning balance of Common Equity?
13.		What is the ending balance of Common Equity?
14.		What is the beginning balance of Total Liabilities?
15.		What is the E.B.I.T.?

19

1-8.

#	Cash	M/S	A/R	Sup	F/A	A/D	=	A/P	N/P	LTD	C/S	R/E	Desc
1	500	400	1000	300	4000	-1500	=	100	800	2000	1000	800	Beg. Bal.
2	5000						=			5000			
3	-4000	4000					=						
4			3000				=					3000	Revenue
5	1000						=					1000	Revenue
6	-2000						=					-2000	Oper. Exp.
7	-1000						=					-1000	Sal & Wag
8	2000		-2000				=						
9				-100			=					-100	Sup. Exp.
10	-2000				2000		=						
11						-400	=					-400	Depr. Exp.
12	-200						=					-200	Tax Exp.
13	1000						=				1000		
14	-100						=					-100	Dividend
15	200	4400	2000	200	6000	-1900	=	100	800	7000	2000	1000	End. Bal.
16	-300	4000	1000	-100	2000	-400		0	0	5000	1000	200	Change

Enter the answer to each question below based on the data above.

1.		What is the Gross Profit?
2.		What is the E.B.I.T.?
3.		What is the Net Income?
4.		What is the Operating Cash Flow?
5.		What is the beginning cash and cash equivalents?
6.		What is the ending cash and cash equivalents?
7.		What is the change in cash and cash equivalents?
8.		What is the Investing Cash Flow?
9.		What is the Financing Cash Flow?
10.		What is the cash collections?
11.		What is the cash impact inventory purchases?
12.		What is the cash impact supplies purchases?
13.		What is the cash impact operating and salary & wages expenses?
14.		What is the cash impact of a change in accounts receivable?
15.		What is the cash impact of a change in accounts payable?

Lesson 2: Time Value of Money (Part 1)

Purpose: Demonstrate that time has an impact on the value of money. Introduce simple tools for calculating the (1) interest rate; (2) number of periods; (3) future value; (4) present value; or the (5) annuity payment.

Application: Use the "TVM" tool found at www.businessallstars.com/calculator to access an excel spreadsheet that can be a model for analyzing the time value of money. The sheet is divided into a right side that calculates one of the five basic inputs for a simple sum and/or annuity. The left side calculates the net present value for a series of uneven cash flows over a selected number of periods or for a indefinite series that will require the calculation of a horizon value.

TVM = Time Value of Money

Name_____   Date_____

Standard Four Function Calculator

F	Inputs	Results
Rate - Interest Rate		
Nper - Number of Periods		
FV - Future Value		
PV - Present Value		
Pmt - Annuity Payment		
Type - Begin = 1; End = 0	0	

Specific Cash Flows Discounted

H Year	Cash Flows		Total FV
0		$ -	$ -
1			$ -
2			$ -
3			$ -
4			$ -
5			$ -
6			$ -
7			$ -
8			$ -
9			$ -
10			$ -
11			$ -

Discount Rate _____

Growth Rate _____

Net Present Value $0.00

Notes:_____

_____

_____

_____

Solving for the **RATE**, the excel function would be:

=rate(nper,pmt,pv,[fv],[type],[guess])

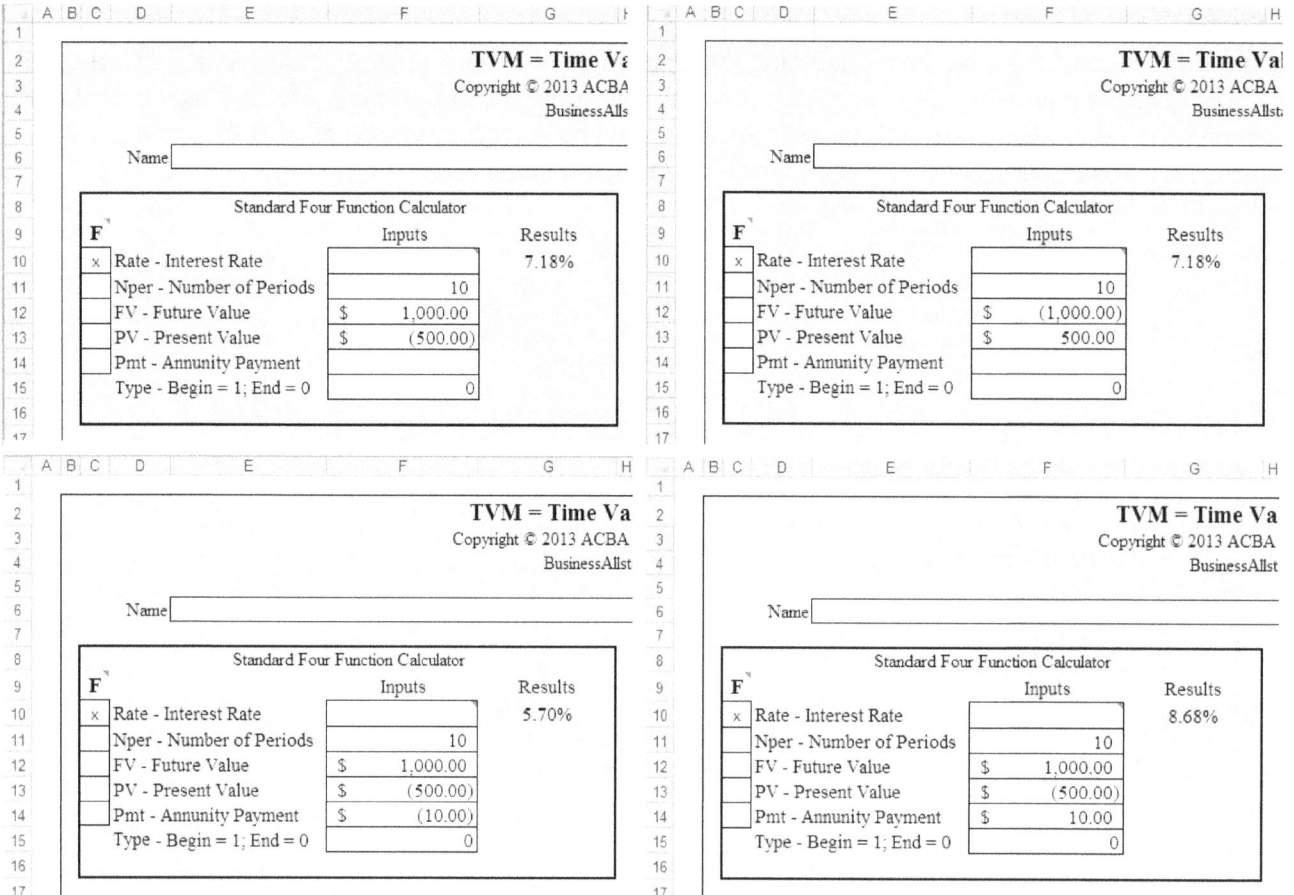

- Option #1 (Top left corner) is for a ten year term, *investing* $500 today and expecting to receive $1,000 at the end of the term. It would require a 7.18% rate.
- Option #2 (Top right corner) is for a ten year term, *receiving* $500 today and expecting to pay $1,000 at the end of the term. It would require a 7.18% rate.
- Option #3 (Bottom left corner) is for a ten year term, investing $500 today, *investing* $10 at the end of every year during the term, and receiving $1,000 at the end of the term. It would require a 5.70% rate.
- Option #4 (Bottom right corner) is for a ten year term, investing $500 today, *receiving* $10 at the end of every year during the term, and receiving $1,000 at the end of the term. It would require a 8.68% rate.

Notes:_____
_____
_____
_____

Solving for the **Number of PERiods**, the excel function would be:

=nper(rate,pmt,pv,]fv],[type])

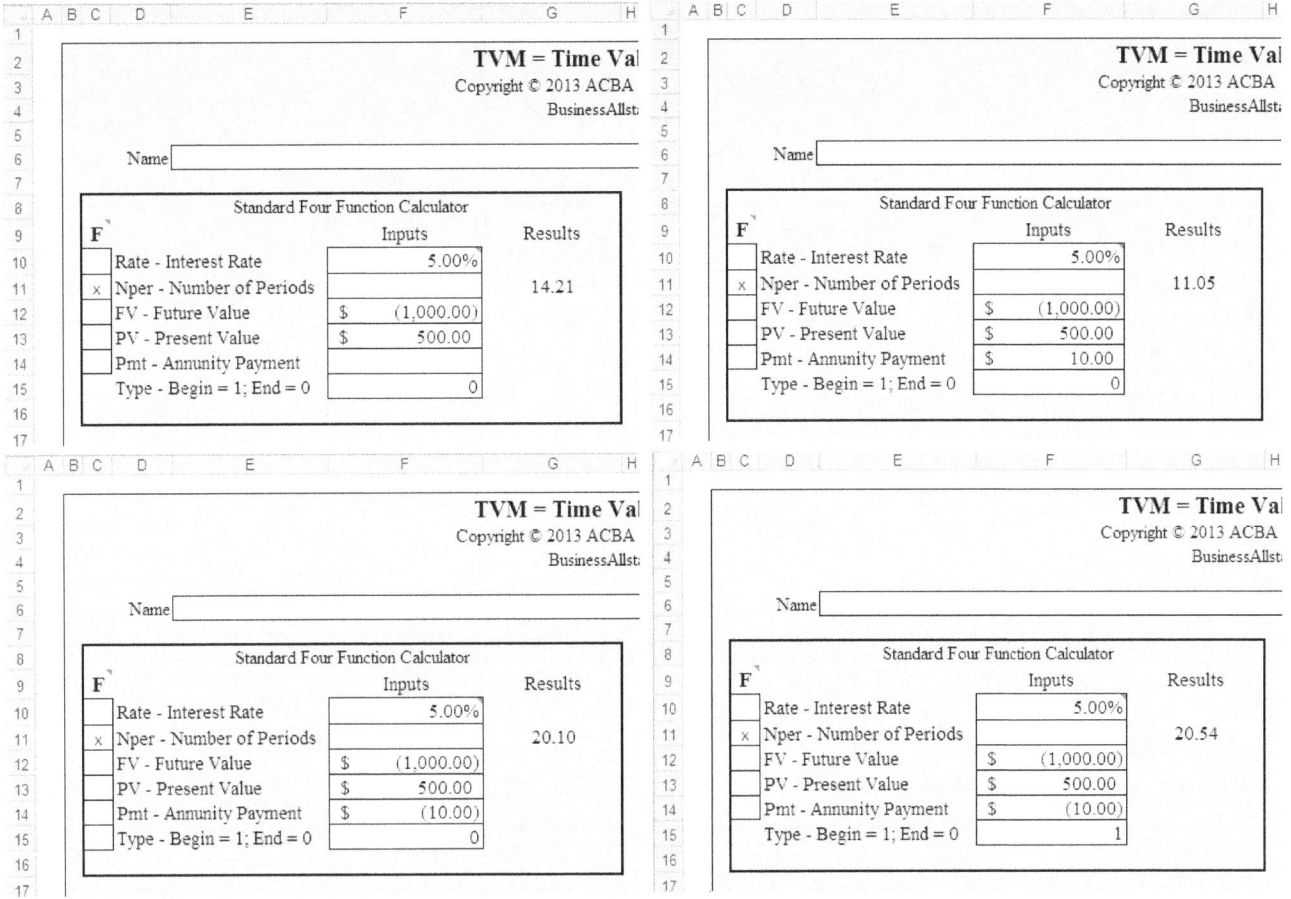

- Option #1 (Top left corner) is at a 5% rate per period, _receiving_ $500 today and expecting to pay $1,000 at the end of the term.
- Option #2 (Top right corner) is at a 5% rate per period, _receiving_ $500 today, expecting to pay $1,000 at the end of the term and receiving $10 at the end of every period during the term.
- Option #3 (Bottom left corner) is at a 5% rate per period, _receiving_ $500 today, expecting to pay $1,000 at the end of the term and paying $10 at the end of every period during the term.
- Option #4 (Bottom right corner) is at a 5% rate per period, _receiving_ $500 today, expecting to pay $1,000 at the end of the term, and paying $10 at the beginning of every period during the term.

Notes:_____

_____

_____

_____

Solving for the **Future Value**, the excel function would be:

=fv(rate,nper,pmt,[pv],[type])

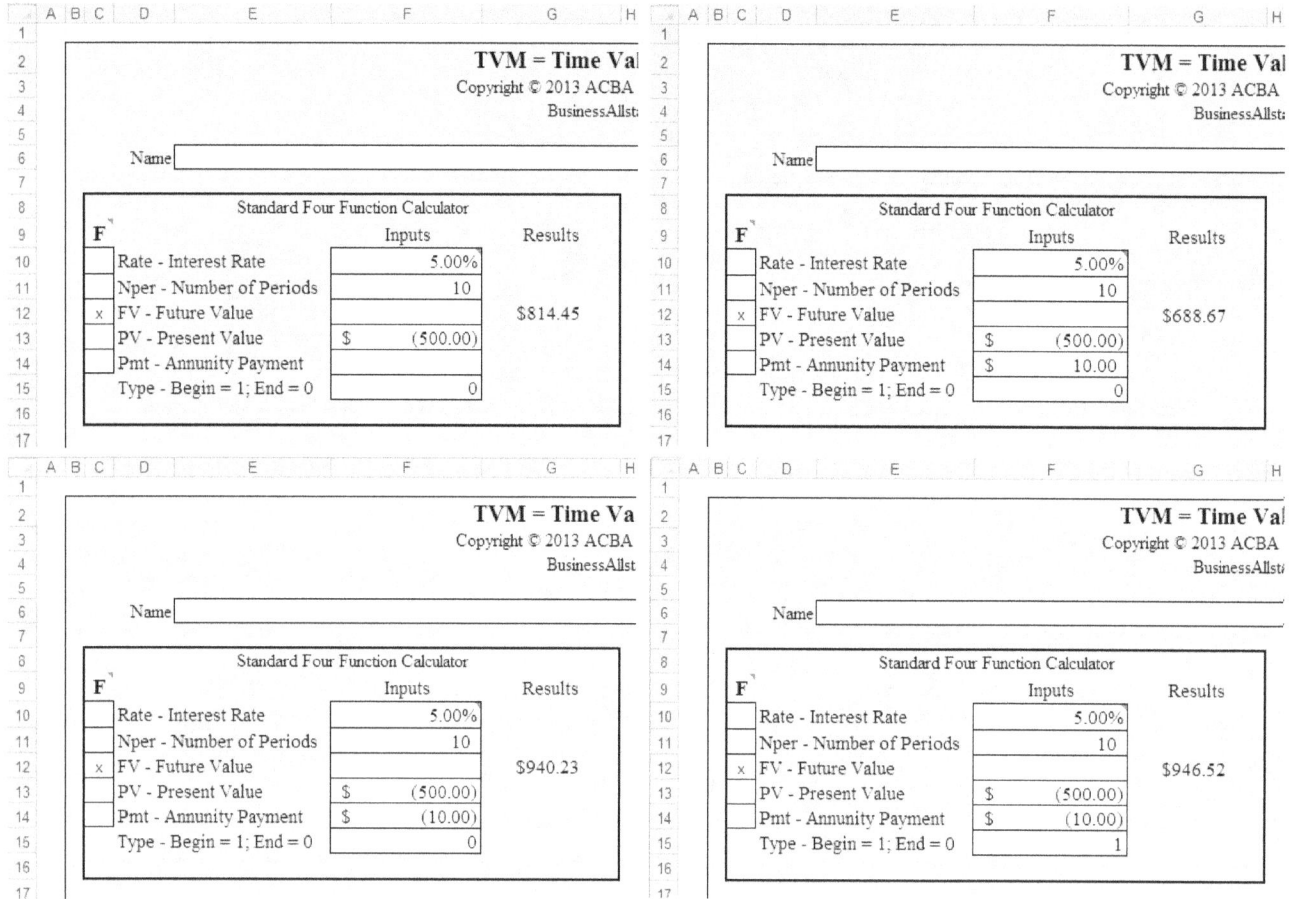

- Option #1 (Top left corner) is at a 5% rate per period, paying $500 today for a term of 10 years.
- Option #2 (Top right corner) is at a 5% rate per period, paying $500 today, receiving $10 at the end of every period during the term for a term of 10 years.
- Option #3 (Bottom left corner) is at a 5% rate per period, paying $500 today, paying $10 at the end of every period during the term for a term of 10 years.
- Option #4 (Bottom right corner) is at a 5% rate per period, paying $500 today, paying $10 at the beginning of every period during the term for a term of 10 years.

Notes:_____

_____

_____

_____

Solving for the **Present Value**, the excel function would be:

$$=pv(rate,nper,pmt,[fv],[type])$$

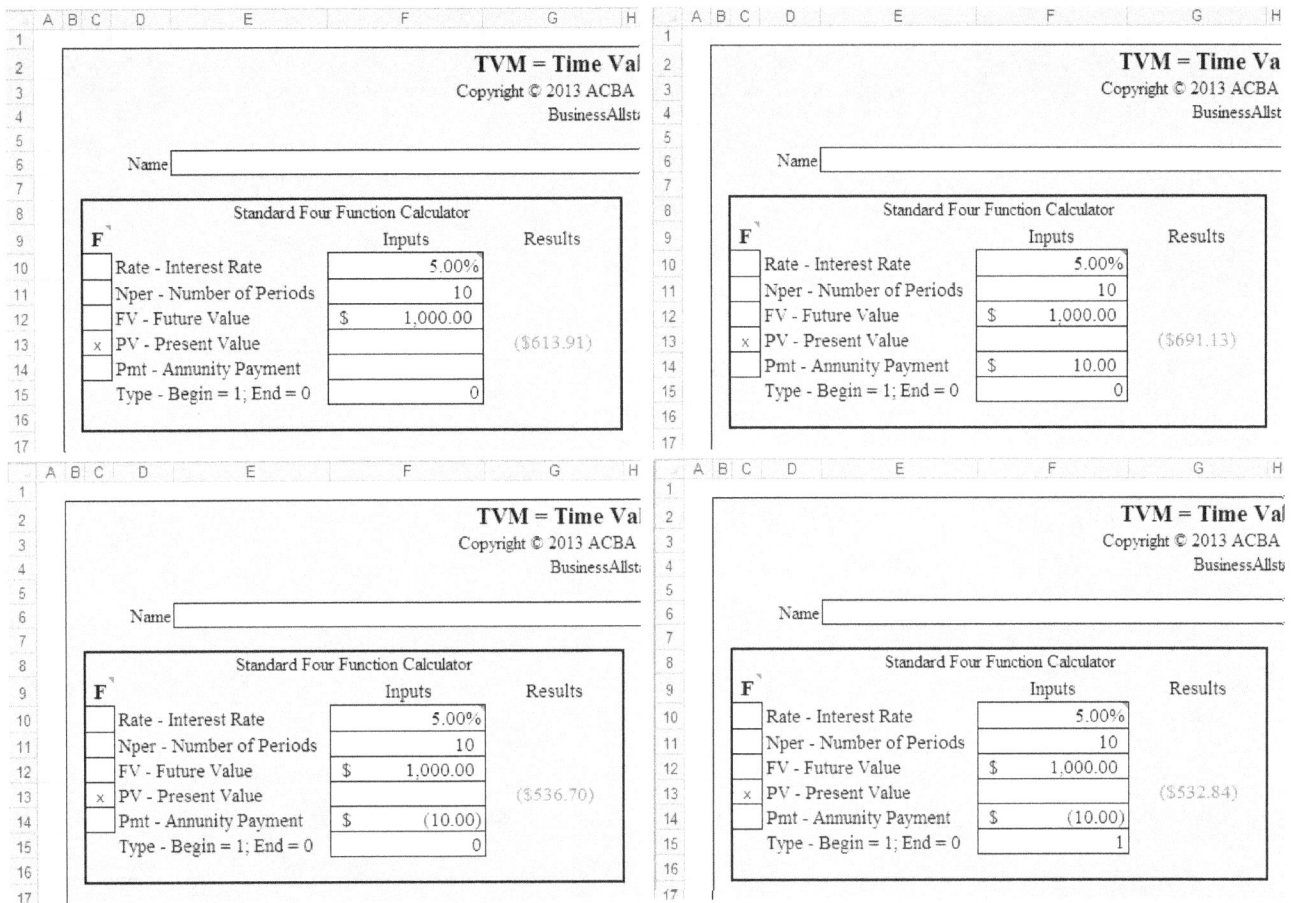

- Option #1 (Top left corner) is at a 5% rate per period, receiving $1,000 at the end of a term of 10 periods.
- Option #2 (Top right corner) is at a 5% rate per period, receiving $10 at the end of each period and $1,000 at the end of a term of 10 periods.
- Option #3 (Bottom left corner) is at a 5% rate per period, paying $10 at the end of each period and receiving $1,000 at the end of a term of 10 periods.
- Option #4 (Bottom right corner) is at a 5% rate per period, paying $10 at the beginning of each period and receiving $1,000 at the end of a term of 10 periods.

Notes:_____

_____

_____

_____

Solving for the **PayMenT,** the excel function would be:

$$=pmt(rate,nper,pv,[fv],[type])$$

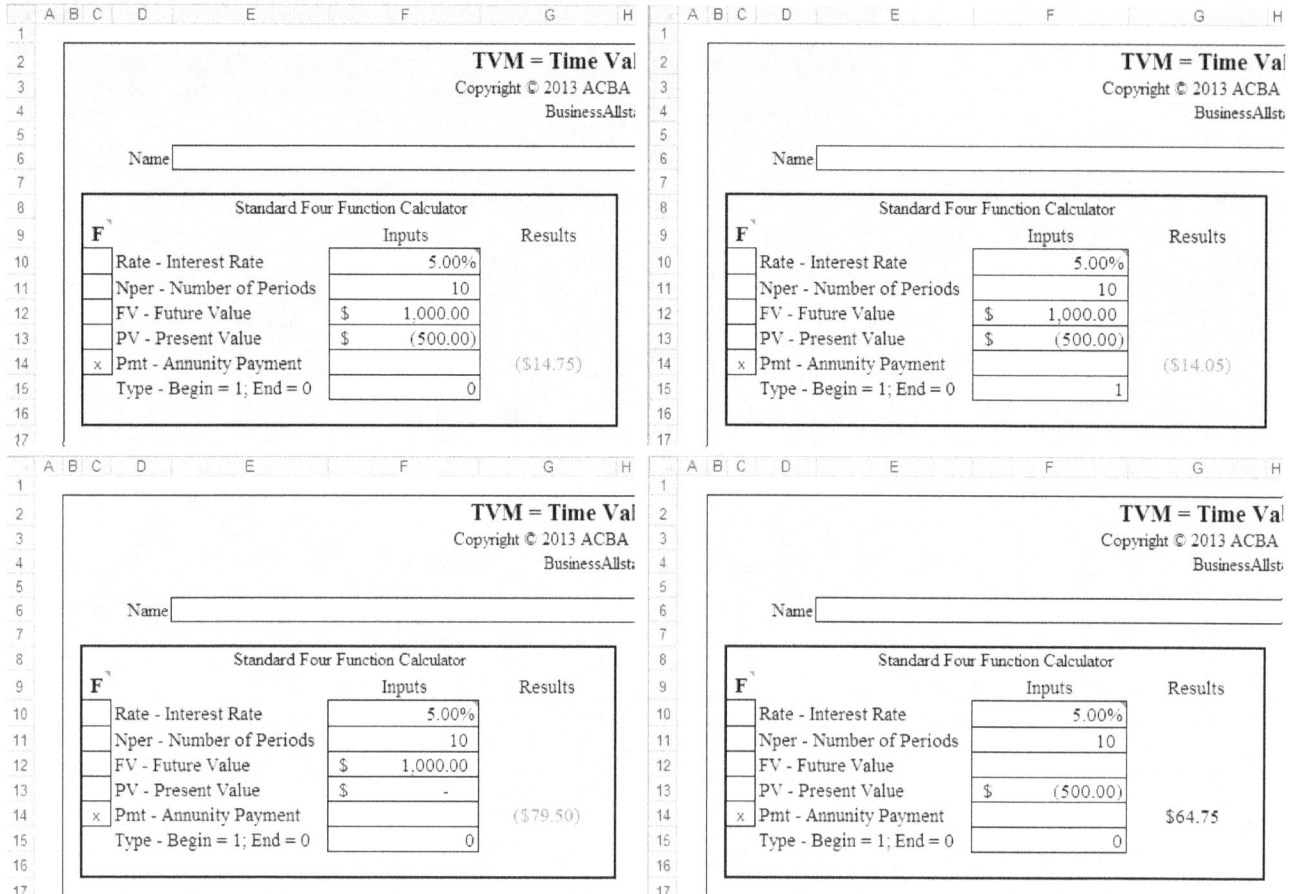

- Option #1 (Top left corner) is at a 5% rate per period, paying $500 today and receiving $1,000 at the end of the term of 10 periods.
- Option #2 (Top right corner) is at a 5% rate per period, paying $500 today and receiving $1,000 at the beginning of the last period in a the term of 10 periods.
- Option #3 (Bottom left corner) is at a 5% rate per period, receiving $1,000 at the end of the term of 10 periods.
- Option #4 (Bottom right corner) is at a 5% rate per period, paying $500 today for a term of 10 periods.

Notes:_____

_____

_____

_____

Solving for the **Net Present Value**, the excel function would be:

$$=npv(rate, value1, [value2], \ldots)$$

Date _____

Specific Cash Flows Discounted

H	Year	Cash Flows		Total FV	
	0	$	-	$	-
	1	$ 100.00		$	100.00
	2	$ 150.00		$	150.00
	3	$ 175.00		$	175.00
	4	$ 200.00		$	200.00
	5	$ 210.00		$	210.00
	6			$	-
	7			$	-
	8			$	-
	9			$	-
	10			$	-
	11			$	-

Discount Rate	10.00%
Growth Rate	5.00%
Net Present Value	$613.35

Date _____

Specific Cash Flows Discounted

H	Year	Cash Flows	Horizon Value	Total FV
x	0	$ -	$ -	$ -
	1	$ 100.00	$ -	$ 100.00
	2	$ 150.00	$ -	$ 150.00
	3	$ 175.00	$ -	$ 175.00
	4	$ 200.00	$ 4,200.00	$ 4,400.00
	5	$ 210.00	$ -	
	6		$ -	
	7		$ -	
	8		$ -	
	9		$ -	
	10		$ -	
	11			

Discount Rate	10.00%
Growth Rate	5.00%
Net Present Value	$3,351.62

- Option #1 (Top left corner) is at a 10% discount rate per period, a growth rate of 5% and cash flows of $100; $150; $175; $200; and $210 for each of the next 5 years respectively. (The growth rate in this case is irrelevant)

- Option #2 (Top right corner) is at a 10% discount rate per period, a growth rate of 5% and cash flows of $100; $150; $175; $200; and $210 for each of the next 5 years respectively. An "x" has been entered in the H cell and so a horizon value is calculated for year 4 based on the cash flow for year 5.

Notes:_____

_____

_____

_____

Lesson 2 Exercises

2-1. Fill in the missing numbers:

	Rate	Nper	FV	PV	Pmt	Type
A	5%	10	$1,000		0	0
B	6%	12	$1,000		200	0
C	5%	20		($500)	0	0
D	7%	15		($500)	($50)	0
E	8%	5		($500)	$50	0
F	2%		$1,000	($300)	0	0
G	3%		($500)	$200	$20	0
H	3%		($500)	$200	$20	1
I		10	($400)	$100	0	0
J		8	($600)	$100	$50	0
K		8	($600)	$100	$50	1
L		5	($400)	0	$50	0
M	9%	10	$1,100	($120)		0
N	9%	10	$1,100	($120)		1
O	10%	9	($800)	$70		0

2-2. Crazy Craig has a pizza joint and has just signed a contract with a local college to provide pizza every Friday at noon in the student union for the next nine months. He is expecting the net profit for each of the next nine month to be: $100; $120; $150; $80; $160; $180; $150; $140; and $110. If his annual cost of financing is 6% (.5% per month), what is the present value of the contract.

2-3. Crazy Craig's pizza has estimated that a contract with the local college to provide pizza every Friday at noon in the student union for the nine months during the fall and spring semesters will eventually result in a long term agreement. He expects about $1,200 in net profit the first year, and $1,500; $1,800; $2,300; $2,500 for the following four years respectively. Then he expects the relationship to continue indefinitely with a growth rate of 3% annually. If his cost of financing is 6% annually, what is the potential value of the contract in today's dollars?

Lesson 3: Time Value of Money (Part 2)

Purpose: Demonstrate an amortization schedule for a loan with its related payments for interest and principal. Also, show how time value of money can be a tool for planning a lifelong investment plan that will lead to a financially secure retirement.

Application: Use the "loan" and "life" tools at www.businessallstars.com/calculator to access an excel spreadsheets that can be used for an amortization schedule where a loan is taken out for up to 36 periods or a model can determine a financial plan for an individual who someday will retire. These are both very specific applications of the time value of money.

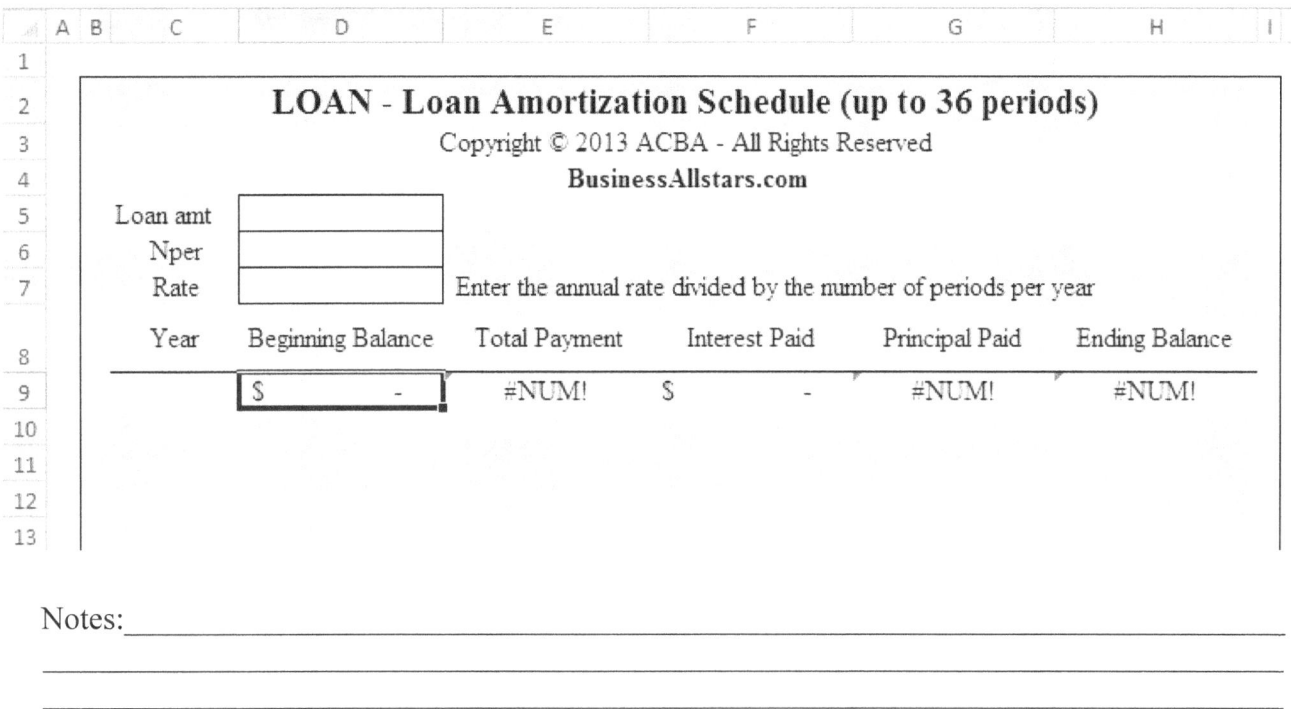

Notes:_____

_____

_____

_____

LOAN - Loan Amortization Schedule (up to 36 periods)

BusinessAllstars.com

Loan amt	$	10,000.00	
Nper		24	
Rate		1.0%	Enter the annual rate divided by the number of periods per year

Year	Beginning Balance	Total Payment	Interest Paid	Principal Paid	Ending Balance
1	$ 10,000.00	$ 470.73	$ 100.00	$ 370.73	$ 9,629.27
2	$ 9,629.27	$ 470.73	$ 96.29	$ 374.44	$ 9,254.82
3	$ 9,254.82	$ 470.73	$ 92.55	$ 378.19	$ 8,876.64
4	$ 8,876.64	$ 470.73	$ 88.77	$ 381.97	$ 8,494.67
5	$ 8,494.67	$ 470.73	$ 84.95	$ 385.79	$ 8,108.88
6	$ 8,108.88	$ 470.73	$ 81.09	$ 389.65	$ 7,719.23
7	$ 7,719.23	$ 470.73	$ 77.19	$ 393.54	$ 7,325.69
8	$ 7,325.69	$ 470.73	$ 73.26	$ 397.48	$ 6,928.21
9	$ 6,928.21	$ 470.73	$ 69.28	$ 401.45	$ 6,526.76
10	$ 6,526.76	$ 470.73	$ 65.27	$ 405.47	$ 6,121.29
11	$ 6,121.29	$ 470.73	$ 61.21	$ 409.52	$ 5,711.77
12	$ 5,711.77	$ 470.73	$ 57.12	$ 413.62	$ 5,298.16
13	$ 5,298.16	$ 470.73	$ 52.98	$ 417.75	$ 4,880.40
14	$ 4,880.40	$ 470.73	$ 48.80	$ 421.93	$ 4,458.47
15	$ 4,458.47	$ 470.73	$ 44.58	$ 426.15	$ 4,032.32
16	$ 4,032.32	$ 470.73	$ 40.32	$ 430.41	$ 3,601.91
17	$ 3,601.91	$ 470.73	$ 36.02	$ 434.72	$ 3,167.19
18	$ 3,167.19	$ 470.73	$ 31.67	$ 439.06	$ 2,728.13
19	$ 2,728.13	$ 470.73	$ 27.28	$ 443.45	$ 2,284.68
20	$ 2,284.68	$ 470.73	$ 22.85	$ 447.89	$ 1,836.79
21	$ 1,836.79	$ 470.73	$ 18.37	$ 452.37	$ 1,384.42
22	$ 1,384.42	$ 470.73	$ 13.84	$ 456.89	$ 927.53
23	$ 927.53	$ 470.73	$ 9.28	$ 461.46	$ 466.07
24	$ 466.07	$ 470.73	$ 4.66	$ 466.07	$ 0.00

Assuming a person takes out a loan with a 24 month payment plan. If the total amount of the loan is $10,000 to be paid back over a 24 month period at a rate of 12% (1% per month), what would be the monthly payment and how much would go toward interest versus principal?

Notes:_____
_____
_____
_____

LIFE is a model that allows the user to play what-if games with expectations about when they will retire and what their life expectancy is. It allows the user to make estimates about the real rate of return on investments during their working career and also during their retirement years. The user must also enter a monthly draw expectation along with how much cash is currently in the bank and what cash they will leave at the time of death. This is an application of the time value of money that is applicable to all.

	A B	C	D	E F	G	H I
1						
2			**LIFE® = Longterm Investment and Financial Estimates**			
3			Copyright © 2013 ACBA - All Rights Reserved			
4			BusinessAllstars.com			
5						
6		Name			Date	
7						
8			Inputs			Outputs
9		Current Age		30	Career Months	420
10		Retirement Age		65	Retirement Months	180
11		Death Age		80	Net Monthly Career Real Inv Rate	1.00%
12		Career Investment Real Return		12%	Net Montly Retirement Real Inv Rate	0.50%
13		Retirement Investment Real Return		6%		
14		Monthly Draw today	S	5,000.00	**Cash needed in Bank at Retirement** S	592,517.57
15		Present Cash in the Bank	S	-	**Career Monthly Investment Begin.** S	92.14
16		Cash left at time of Death	S	-		
17						
18						

Assuming a person is currently 30 years of age, plans to retire at age 65 with a life expectancy of 80. It is also assumed that person can earn 12% annually on their investments during their working career and 6% annually during retirement. If that person would like to retire with a monthly income from a retirement plan of $5,000 per month in today's dollars how much cash would they need in the bank upon retirement. Solving for the **Present** Value of a monthly payout after retirement:

$$=pv(rate,nper,pmt,[fv],[type])$$

Once the total amount in the bank is determined then the person would solve for the monthly **Payment** required during a working career to generate the retirement target amount:

$$=pmt(rate,nper,pv,[fv],[type])$$

Notes:_____

_____

_____

_____

Lesson 3 Exercises

3-1. Complete the Loan model for a loan of $50,000 to be repaid over a period of 24 months at a rate of 6% annual interest.

3-2. Create a spreadsheet for a loan repayment plan where a $100,000 loan is to be repaid for a period of 15 years with monthly payments. The interest is a 3% annual rate.

3-3. Suppose a person is 22 years old, expects to retire at age 70 and live to be 90. In today's dollars they would like to retire and receive $5,000 per month. They presently have no cash in the bank and don't expect to leave anything at the time of their death.

Career Investment Real Return	Retirement Investment Real Return	Cash needed in the Bank at Retirement	Career Monthly Investment (Begin)
12%	6%		
12%	5%		
10%	5%		
10%	4%		
8%	4%		
8%	3%		
6%	3%		
6%	2%		

Lesson 4: The SEC and CEO models

Purpose: Show how to read and evaluate the reports filed by the company with the Securities and Exchange Commission and other sources.

Application: Use the "SEC" and "CEO" tools at www.businessallstars.com/calculator and the data from the 10-K filing with the SEC (Securities and Exchange Commission) and information found at www.finance.yahoo.com . Two companies have been selected for analysis (1) Dollar General Corporation (DG) and (2) Family Dollar Stores Inc. (FDO).

Access to the SEC filing of the 10-K report is gained by going to www.finance.yahoo.com and clicking on the SEC Filing menu item on the left. Then locate the most recent 10-K form for the company from the list offered and click on the "Full Filing at EDGAR Online." Item 1 titled "BUSINESS" gives a description of the business the company is pursuing. As the student reads the section the student will attempt to complete the SEC form from www.businessallstars.com/calculator.

Order Book	
Options	
Historical Prices	

Dollar General Corporation (DG) - NYSE

51.18 ↓0.02(0.04%) Jun 14, 4:00PM EDT | After Hours : **51.18** 0.00 (0.00%) Jun 14, 5:27PM EI

CHARTS	
Interactive	
Basic Chart	
Basic Tech. Analysis	

SEC Filings   Get SEC Filing

The DG Annual Report is now available. Free Annual Report

NEWS & INFO	
Headlines	
Press Releases	
Company Events	
Message Boards	
Market Pulse	

Recent Filings

Date	Form	Title
Jun 3, 2013	8-K	Results of Operations and Financial Condition, Submission of Matters to a Vot Summary - Full Filing at EDGAR Online(295kb)
Jun 3, 2013	10-Q	Quarterly Report Summary - Full Filing at EDGAR Online(4mb)
Apr 10, 2013	8-K	Entry into a Material Definitive Agreement, Termination of a Material Definit Summary - Full Filing at EDGAR Online(2mb)
Apr 1, 2013	8-K	Entry into a Material Definitive Agreement, Other Events, Financial Statement Summary - Full Filing at EDGAR Online(454kb)
Mar 24, 2013	8-K	Results of Operations and Financial Condition, Change in Directors or Princip Summary - Full Filing at EDGAR Online(424kb)
Mar 24, 2013	10-K	Annual Report Summary - Full Filing at EDGAR Online(7mb)

COMPANY	
Profile	
Key Statistics	
▶ SEC Filings	
Competitors	
Industry	
Components	
ANALYST COVERAGE	
Analyst Opinion	
Analyst Estimates	
Research Reports	

http://yahoo.brand.edgar-online.com/DisplayFiling.aspx?dcn=0001047469-13-003283

SEC- Business Scorecard

Student [   ]   Co Ticker [DG   ]   Score [32]

Clicking on a value box next to an answer will award those points for the respective selection
A total score for the form will not show until all questions have been answered.
The maximum score achievable is 32.

1. [4]   How many years has the company been in business?
   ○ Less than 10 years   ○ 10 to 30 years   ○ 30 to 70 years   ● 70 or more years
   ○ It can't be determined

2. [4]   The company is active in which geographic market?
   ○ Metro   ○ State   ○ Region   ● Nation   ○ Continent   ○ Hemisphere   ○ World
   ○ It can't be determined

3. [4]   Typical customers are catergorized as
   ○ Exclusive & Specialty   ○ Targeted & Lifestyle   ● Price & Value
   ○ It can't be determined

4. [4]   Based on McKinsey's the company's most important growth strategy is
   New:
   ○ market arenas   ○ industry structure   ○ geographies   ○ delivery approaches   ○ products
   Existing:
   ○ products to new customers   ● products to existing customers
   ○ It can't be determined

5. [4]   Based on McKinsey's the company's proposed method for achieving strategic growth is
   ○ Acquisitions   ○ Joint Ventures   ○ Minority Stakes
   ○ Strategic Alliances   ○ Marketing Partnerships   ● Organic Investment
   ○ It can't be determined

6. [4]   The company's competitive advantage is strength relative to?
   ○ New competition   ○ Substitutions   ○ Customers   ● Suppliers   ○ Existing competition
   ○ It can't be determined

7. [4]   Based on Peter Lynch's categories the company falls into which group?
   ○ Slow Grower   ● Stalwart (medium growth)   ○ Fast Grower
   ○ Cyclical (regular ups and downs)   ○ Turnaround   ○ Asset-play (hidden)
   ○ It can't be determined

8. [4]   The company's strength is its
   ○ Marketing   ○ Leadership   ○ Systems   ● Products   ○ Loyalty
   ○ It can't be determined

Articles:
McKinsey   Porter   Lynch

Information for the SEC – Business Scorecard came from the 10-K filed with the Securities and Exchange Commission as quoted below:

Our History

J.L. Turner founded our Company in 1939 as J.L. Turner and Son, Wholesale.

General

We are the largest discount retailer in the United States by number of stores, with 10,557 stores located in 40 states as of March 1, 2013

We offer a broad selection ... high quality national brands from leading manufacturers, as well as comparable quality private brand selections with prices at substantial discounts to national brands. We offer our merchandise at everyday low prices (typically $10 or less) through our convenient small-box locations, with selling space averaging approximately 7,300 square feet.

Our Growth Strategy

We believe that our strategy and execution capabilities will allow us to capitalize on the considerable growth opportunities afforded by our business model. Specifically, we believe we continue to have significant opportunities to drive profitable growth through increasing same-store sales, expanding our operating profit rate and growing our store base.

Substantial Growth Opportunities. We believe we have significant long-term growth potential in the U.S. We have identified significant opportunities to add new stores in both existing and new markets. In addition, we have opportunities within our existing store base to relocate or remodel to better serve our customers. As part of our growth strategy, we are developing and testing new store formats, with a current focus on providing customers convenient access to more affordable perishable food items. See "Our Growth Strategy" for additional details.

The Dollar General Store

Our recent store growth is summarized in the following table:

Year	Stores at Beginning of Year	Stores Opened	Stores Closed	Net Store Increase	Stores at End of Year
2010	8,828	600	56	544	9,372
2011	9,372	625	60	565	9,937
2012	9,937	625	56	569	10,506

Our Business Model

Our long history of profitable growth is founded on a commitment to a relatively simple business model: providing a broad base of customers with their basic everyday and household needs, supplemented with a variety of general merchandise items, at everyday low prices in conveniently located, small-box stores. We continually evaluate the needs and demands of our customers and modify our merchandise selections and pricing accordingly, while remaining focused on increasing profitability for our shareholders.

Notes:_____

_____

_____

_____

35

Family Dollar Stores Inc. (FDO) was also examined relative to their SEC filing:

Family Dollar Stores Inc. (FDO) - NYSE

63.23 ↑0.52(0.83%) Jun 14, 4:02PM EDT | After Hours : **63.23** 0.00 (0.00%) Jun 14, 5:27PM

SEC Filings

Get SEC Fili

The FDO Annual Report is now available. Free Annual Report

Recent Filings

Date	Form	Title
Apr 28, 2013	8-K	Change in Directors or Principal Officers, Financial Statements and Exhi Summary - Full Filing at EDGAR Online(16kb)
Apr 9, 2013	8-K	Results of Operations and Financial Condition, Regulation FD Disclosure, Summary - Full Filing at EDGAR Online(194kb)
Apr 9, 2013	10-Q	Quarterly Report Summary - Full Filing at EDGAR Online(2mb)
Jan 22, 2013	8-K	Submission of Matters to a Vote of Security Holders, Other Events, Finan Summary - Full Filing at EDGAR Online(52kb)
Jan 2, 2013	8-K	Change in Directors or Principal Officers, Financial Statements and Exhi Summary - Full Filing at EDGAR Online(109kb)
Jan 2, 2013	10-Q	Quarterly Report Summary - Full Filing at EDGAR Online(2mb)
Nov 15, 2012	8-K	Entry into a Material Definitive Agreement, Material Modification to Rig Summary - Full Filing at EDGAR Online(27kb)
Nov 8, 2012	8-K	Other Events Summary - Full Filing at EDGAR Online(21kb)
Oct 18, 2012	10-K	Annual Report Summary - Full Filing at EDGAR Online(5mb)

SEC- Business Scorecard

Student		Co Ticker	FDO	Score	32

Clicking on a value box next to an answer will award those points for the respective selection
A total score for the form will not show until all questions have been answered.
The maximum score achievable is 32.

1. `4` How many years has the company been in business?
   ○ Less than 10 years   ○ 10 to 30 years   ● 30 to 70 years   ○ 70 or more years
   ○ It can't be determined

2. `4` The company is active in which geographic market?
   ○ Metro   ○ State   ○ Region   ● Nation   ○ Continent   ○ Hemisphere   ○ World
   ○ It can't be determined

3. `4` Typical customers are catergorized as
   ○ Exclusive & Specialty   ○ Targeted & Lifestyle   ● Price & Value
   ○ It can't be determined

4. `4` Based on McKinsey's the company's most important growth strategy is
   New:
   ○ market arenas   ○ industry structure   ○ geographies   ○ delivery approaches   ○ products
   Existing:
   ○ products to new customers   ● products to existing customers
   ○ It can't be determined

5. `4` Based on McKinsey's the company's proposed method for achieving strategic growth is
   ○ Acquisitions   ○ Joint Ventures   ○ Minority Stakes
   ○ Strategic Alliances   ○ Marketing Partnerships   ● Organic Investment
   ○ It can't be determined

6. `4` The company's competitive advantage is strength relative to?
   ○ New competition   ○ Substitutions   ○ Customers   ● Suppliers   ○ Existing competition
   ○ It can't be determined

7. `4` Based on Peter Lynch's categories the company falls into which group?
   ○ Slow Grower   ● Stalwart (medium growth)   ○ Fast Grower
   ○ Cyclical (regular ups and downs)   ○ Turnaround   ○ Asset-play (hidden)
   ○ It can't be determined

8. `4` The company's strength is its
   ○ Marketing   ○ Leadership   ○ Systems   ○ Products   ● Loyalty
   ○ It can't be determined

Articles:
McKinsey   Porter   Lynch

ITEM 1. BUSINESS (Family Dollar Stores, Inc.)

General Overview

We operate a chain of more than 7,400 general merchandise retail discount stores in 45 states, providing value-conscious consumers with a selection of competitively priced merchandise in convenient neighborhood stores.

We opened our first Family Dollar store in Charlotte, North Carolina, in 1959.

Our Mission and Vision

Our mission is to provide our customers with a compelling place to shop, our team members with a compelling place to work, and our investors with a compelling place to invest. Our vision is to be the best, small-format convenience and value retailer serving the needs of families in our neighborhoods.

Our Growth Strategy

We believe that balancing initiatives targeted to deliver short-term financial results with investments that may require longer-term development will help us weather difficult macro-environments and enable us to achieve our long-term financial goals. During fiscal 2012 , we focused on achieving our four corporate goals: build customer loyalty and experience; deliver profitable sales growth; drive continuous improvement; and develop diverse, high performing teams. These goals are designed to drive both short-term and longer-term financial results.

Deliver profitable sales growth

Several years ago, we slowed new store growth to focus more on improving returns in existing stores and the chain overall. Over this period, we completed an end-to-end re-engineering of our merchandising and supply chain processes, enhanced productivity of our store teams, refreshed our store technology platform, and created a store layout for new stores that is more convenient and easier to shop. As a result of these investments, we upgraded our operational capabilities, increased profitability, gained productivity, and expanded our financial returns. More importantly, these investments have provided us with a strong foundation to accelerate revenue growth.

Private brands represent an opportunity to increase sales and profitability. To drive this growth, we added nearly 400 private brand consumables SKUs to our assortment in fiscal 2012 . Building on this momentum, in fiscal 2013 we intend to increase our penetration of private brands even further, with a continued focus on expanding our assortment of private brands consumables. We expect to launch new brands that will offer our customers more quality and value while also refreshing a few of our existing brands to broaden their appeal. And, we intend to drive greater awareness of our private brands program through increased marketing and visual merchandising support.

In fiscal 2012 , approximately 24% of our purchased merchandise (at cost) was manufactured overseas. While we continue to rely extensively on third parties to help us procure this merchandise, we are progressively moving toward a more efficient, direct model. In fiscal 2012 , we expanded our teams in our Hong Kong and Shenzhen, China offices. In fiscal 2013, we expect to open an office in Shanghai, China. Today, these teams are strengthening and expanding our supplier network. We also invested in new tools to help us manage the product development cycle better. As a result of these investments, we increased our direct imports by more than 40% in fiscal 2012 , as compared to fiscal 2011. In fiscal 2013 , we plan to continue to expand our Global Sourcing teams, develop stronger processes to help us integrate our sourcing activities with our category management efforts, and continue to expand our supplier network.

CEO Scorecard

Student [   ]   Co Ticker [DG]   CEO [Richard W. Dreiling]   Calc. [22]

Clicking on a value box next to an answer will award those points for the respective selection
A total score for the form will not show until all questions have been answered.
The maximum score achievable is 32.

1. [3] The CEO age in years is closest to?
   ○ 35 [1]   ○ 40 [2]   ● 45 [3]   ○ **50** [4]   ○ 55 [3]   ○ 60 [2]   ○ 65 [1]

1. [1] The CEO's tenure at the company in years is closest to?
   ● 5 [1]   ○ 10 [2]   ○ 15 [3]   ○ **20** [4]   ○ 25 [3]   ○ 30 [2]   ○ 35 [1]

3. [4] What was the CEOs background?
   ○ Human Resource Management [1]
   ○ Information [2]
   ○ Finance [3]
   ● **Operations** [4]
   ○ Engineering [3]
   ○ Marketing [2]
   ○ Law [1]

4. [3] How many other employers has the CEO worked for?
   ○ 0 [2]   ○ 1 [4]   ● 2 [3]   ○ 3 [2]   ○ 4 or more [1]

5. [2] Approximately how long has the CEO been the CEO of this company?
   ○ 0 [2]   ○ 2 [4]   ○ 4 [3]   ● 6 [2]   ○ 8 [1]   ○ 10 or more [0]

6. [2] From reading the 10-K and news articles does the CEO have a BIG GROWTH IDEA?
   ○ Yes [4]   ● It's hard to tell [2]   ○ No [0]

7. [4] Has the company had a strong EVA history in recent years?
   ● Yes [4]   ○ It's hard to tell [2]   ○ No [0]

8. [3] Generally, how would you rate the CEO on the following characteristics
   (from "How to think like a CEO" by D. A. Benton,
   Published by Business Plus, New York, 1996):

1. Secure in Self	12. A Tad Theatrical
2. In control of Attitude	13. Detail Oriented
3. Tenacious	14. Good at their job and willing to lead
4. Continuously Improving	15. Fighters for their people
5. Honest and ethical	16. Willing to admit mistakes, yet unapologetic
6. Thinking before talking	17. Straightforward
7. Original	18. Nice
8. Publicly Modest	19. Inquisitive
9. Aware of Style	20. Competitive
10. Gutsy/A Little Wild	21. Flexible
11. Humorous	22. Good storyteller

   ○ Very High [4]   ● High [3]   ○ Normal [2]   ○ Low [1]   ○ Very Low [0]

Articles:
Forbes   Barrons   Traits   Growth   Telegraph   Glassdoor

January 14, 2008
Dollar General Names Richard W. Dreiling CEO
Veteran Retailer Takes the Helm at Largest Small-box Retailer in the U.S.

GOODLETTSVILLE, Tenn., Jan 14, 2008 (BUSINESS WIRE) -- Dollar General today announced that Richard W. Dreiling has been appointed CEO of the 8,000+ store discount chain, effective January 21. Dreiling, a 38-year veteran retailer, most recently served as chairman, president and CEO of New York-based Duane Reade, the largest drug store chain in the New York City metropolitan area. Prior to his tenure at Duane Reade, Dreiling served in senior leadership roles with Safeway, Inc. and Longs Drug Stores.

"Dollar General has made excellent progress in recent months, and I believe there are exciting opportunities to extend the company's record of innovation in the small-box discounting segment," said Dreiling. "I look forward to joining the Dollar General team and will work aggressively to enhance the brand and strengthen the company's position as a leader in serving cost-conscious shoppers who value convenience."

Dreiling, 54, served 33 years at Safeway in a number of leadership roles, including executive vice president of marketing, manufacturing and distribution and president of the Von's division. Immediately prior to joining Duane Reade, Dreiling was the executive vice president and COO of Longs Drug Stores Corporation.

"Rick ranks among the retail industry's outstanding executives, and he has a long and successful track record. He brings to Dollar General extensive retail experience and expertise in store operations, merchandising, marketing and distribution. He believes in the brand and understands what it means to our customers, and he will ensure we maintain the business and financial discipline necessary to take Dollar General to the next level," said Mike Calbert, Dollar General's chairman, and member of Kohlberg Kravis Roberts & Co., which acquired Dollar General in July, 2007.

David Bere, Dollar General's president and COO who served as interim CEO, will continue to serve the company as president and COO.

"We are grateful for David's service as interim CEO during our search process," said Calbert. "Under his leadership, we have had strong financial performance and have made significant progress in executing our strategic initiatives. Rick and I look forward to working with him to continue building the value of Dollar General."

About Dollar General

Dollar General is a leading discount retailer with more than 8,000 neighborhood stores. Dollar General helps shoppers Save time, Save money(R) by offering national branded items that are frequently used and replenished such as food, snacks, health and beauty aids, cleaning supplies, basic apparel, house wares and seasonal items at everyday low prices in convenient neighborhood stores. Dollar General is among the largest retailers of top-quality products made by America's most trusted manufacturers such as Proctor & Gamble, Kimberly Clark, Unilever, Kellogg's, General Mills, Nabisco, and Fruit of the Loom. [1]

Richard Dreiling
Chief Executive Officer, Dollar General Corp.
Richard W. "Rick" Dreiling joined Dollar General in January 2008 as CEO, and was elected chairman of the board in December 2008. Since 2005, Dreiling had been with Duane Reade Holdings Inc. as chairman and CEO. Duane Reade is the leading drug store chain in the New York City metropolitan area.

---

[1] http://investor.shareholder.com/dollar/releasedetail.cfm?releaseid=286794

In 2003, prior to his tenure with Duane Reade, Dreiling served as executive vice president and chief operating officer of Longs Drug Stores Corporation, a chain of retail drug stores on the West Coast and Hawaii. Before that, he was executive vice president of marketing, manufacturing and distribution of Safeway Inc. a food and drug retailer. Earlier still, he served as president of Vons, a southern California division of Safeway Inc.

Dreiling earned a bachelor's degree in industrial relations from Rockhurst University in Missouri. He began his career in 1969 as a part-time clerk with Safeway Inc. in Kansas, where he worked his way through the retail ranks before being promoted to president of Vons in 1998. Dreiling serves on the board of the National Association of Chain Drug Stores (NACDS) and the board of directors of Chain Drug Consortium, LLC. Dreiling was a finalist in Ernst & Young's 2007 Entrepreneur of the Year Awards for the Metro New York area. In October 2007, Dreiling received the Jacob K. Javits Lifetime Achievement Award in recognition of his efforts to raise awareness for the ALS Association and to support its work to find a cure for the disease. He was also a recipient of the 2006 Human Rights Award, given by the Jewish Labor Committee, in recognition of his efforts to promote the shared social justice agenda between the AJC and the trade union movement; he was honored again in October 2006 as their "Person of the Year."[2]

Notes:_____

_____

_____

_____

[2] http://topics.wsj.com/person/D/richard-dreiling/4319

CEO Scorecard

Student		Co Ticker	FDO	CEO	Howard Levine		Calc.	22

**Clicking on a value box next to an answer will award those points for the respective selection
A total score for the form will not show until all questions have been answered.
The maximum score achievable is 32.**

1. [4] The CEO age in years is closest to?
   ○ 35 [1]   ○ 40 [2]   ○ 45 [3]   ● **50** [4]   ○ 55 [3]   ○ 60 [2]   ○ 65 [1]

1. [4] The CEO's tenure at the company in years is closest to?
   ○ 5 [1]   ○ 10 [2]   ○ 15 [3]   ● **20** [4]   ○ 25 [3]   ○ 30 [2]   ○ 35 [1]

3. [2] What was the CEOs background?
   ○ Human Resource Management [1]
   ○ Information [2]
   ○ Finance [3]
   ○ **Operations** [4]
   ○ Engineering [3]
   ● Marketing [2]
   ○ Law [1]

4. [3] How many other employers has the CEO worked for?
   ○ 0 [2]   ○ 1 [4]   ● 2 [3]   ○ 3 [2]   ○ 4 or more [1]

5. [0] Approximately how long has the CEO been the CEO of this company?
   ○ 0 [2]   ○ 2 [4]   ○ 4 [3]   ○ 6 [2]   ○ 8 [1]   ● 10 or more [0]

6. [2] From reading the 10-K and news articles does the CEO have a BIG GROWTH IDEA?
   ○ Yes [4]   ● It's hard to tell [2]   ○ No [0]

7. [4] Has the company had a strong EVA history in recent years?
   ● Yes [4]   ○ It's hard to tell [2]   ○ No [0]

8. [3] Generally, how would you rate the CEO on the following characteristics
   (from "How to think like a CEO" by D. A. Benton,
   Published by Business Plus, New York, 1996):

1. Secure in Self	12. A Tad Theatrical
2. In control of Attitude	13. Detail Oriented
3. Tenacious	14. Good at their job and willing to lead
4. Continuously Improving	15. Fighters for their people
5. Honest and ethical	16. Willing to admit mistakes, yet unapologetic
6. Thinking before talking	17. Straightforward
7. Original	18. Nice
8. Publicly Modest	19. Inquisitive
9. Aware of Style	20. Competitive
10. Gutsy/A Little Wild	21. Flexible
11. Humorous	22. Good storyteller

   ○ Very High [4]   ● High [3]   ○ Normal [2]   ○ Low [1]   ○ Very Low [0]

Articles:
Forbes   Barrons   Traits   Growth   Telegraph   Glassdoor

Howard Levine
Chairman and chief executive officer, Family Dollar Stores Inc.
Mr. Levine has been the Chairman of the Board since January 2003 and Chief Executive Officer of Family Dollar since August 1998. Mr. Levine was employed by the Company in various capacities in the Merchandising Department from 1981 to 1987, including employment as Senior Vice President – Merchandising and Advertising. From 1988 to 1992, Mr. Levine was President of Best Price Clothing Stores, Inc., a chain of ladies' apparel stores. He rejoined the Company in April 1996, and was elected Vice President – General Merchandise Manager: Softlines in April 1996, Senior Vice President – Merchandising and Advertising in September 1996, President and Chief Operating Officer in April 1997, and Chief Executive Officer in August 1998. In addition, Mr. Levine serves as a member on the Equity Award Committee. He is the son of Mr. Leon Levine, the Founder of the Company who retired in January 2003.[3]

Howard Levine: A family man[4]

By David Perlmutt
Posted Tuesday, Jun 21, 2011

"Howard has a deep commitment to making sure that business thrives and grows," Daniel Levine says.

As board chairman and Family Dollar's largest single shareholder, Howard recently led the rebuff of a $7.6 billion takeover bid by a New York hedge fund. In leading the charge, he put aside his family ties, he says. "It was a business decision," he says. "The fact that I grew up in the business, sure I had personal feelings. But they weren't relevant to this business decision. I had to do the right thing for the business and the shareholders."

Like his father, Howard is hands-on and competitive at work, a man bent on expanding the empire. Daily, he eats lunch in his office, inviting two or three employees from various parts of the company to join him. It's a way to stay in touch.

He's seen as a methodical CEO, sweating details and making decisions only after all options are weighed. He starts each morning reading the previous day's sales, and, like his father did, often drops in on stores unannounced to see what customers are buying and thinking. He's also known to visit stores of his company's biggest competitor, Dollar General.

"He enjoys being a Family Dollar customer," says Jim Kelly, Family Dollar's president and Howard's closest advisor. "It helps him understand how successful we're being here as an organization."

"My father has a style, I have a different style. I'm a private man."

Lesson 4 Exercises

4-1. Complete the SEC and CEO models for the company your instructor selects by extracting data from the most recent fiscal year end 10-K filed with the Securities and Exchange Commission and data as found on the internet or other sources.

4-2. Complete the SEC and CEO models for a public company that you have selected as the entity you intend to analyze throughout the rest of this course. Extract data from the most recent fiscal year end 10-K filed with the Securities and Exchange Commission and data as found on the internet or other sources.

Lesson 5: Financial Statements

[3] http://topics.wsj.com/person/l/howard-levine/746
[4] http://www.charlotteobserver.com/2011/06/21/2395861/howard-levine-a-family-man.html

Purpose: To show students how the basic financial are presented by various services from the initial SEC filings to secondary sources that process the data for presentation and analysis.

Application: Locate and use the financial statements presented by two companies in the free-edgar data base. The statements will include the fiscal year end Consolidated Statement of Income, Unaudited Quarterly Financial Data, Consolidated Balance Sheet, Consolidated Statement of Cash Flows, and the Market for Registrant's Common Equity.

DOLLAR GENERAL CORPORATION AND SUBSIDIARIES

CONSOLIDATED STATEMENTS OF INCOME

(In thousands, except per share amounts)

	For the Year Ended		
	February 1, 2013	February 3, 2012	January 28, 2011
Net sales	$ 16,022,128	$ 14,807,188	$ 13,035,000
Cost of goods sold	10,936,727	10,109,278	8,858,444
Gross profit	5,085,401	4,697,910	4,176,556
Selling. general and administrative expenses	3,430,125	3,207,106	2,902,491
Operating profit	1,655,276	1,490,804	1,274,065
Interest expense	127,926	204,900	273,992
Other (income) expense	29,956	60,615	15,101
Income before income taxes	1,497,394	1,225,289	984,972
Income tax expense	544,732	458,604	357,115
Net income	$ 952,662	$ 766,685	$ 627,857
Earnings per share:			
Basic	$ 2.87	$ 2.25	$ 1.84
Diluted	$ 2.85	$ 2.22	$ 1.82
Weighted average shares:			
Basic	332,254	341,234	341,047
Diluted	334,469	345,117	344,800

http://yahoo.brand.edgar-online.com/displayfilinginfo.aspx?FilingID=9181907-221510-451460&type=sect&dcn=0001047469-13-003283

DOLLAR GENERAL CORPORATION AND SUBSIDIARIES

CONSOLIDATED BALANCE SHEETS

(In thousands, except per share amounts)

	February 1, 2013	February 3, 2012
ASSETS		
Current assets:		
Cash and cash equivalents	$ 140,809	$ 126,126
Merchandise inventories	2,397,175	2,009,206
Prepaid expenses and other current assets	139,129	139,742
Total current assets	2,677,113	2,275,074
Net property and equipment	2,088,665	1,794,960
Goodwill	4,338,589	4,338,589
Other intangible assets, net	1,219,543	1,235,954
Other assets, net	43,772	43,943
Total assets	$ 10,367,682	$ 9,688,520
LIABILITIES AND SHAREHOLDERS' EQUITY		
Current liabilities:		
Current portion of long-term obligations	$ 892	$ 590
Accounts payable	1,261,607	1,064,087
Accrued expenses and other	357,438	397,075
Income taxes payable	95,387	44,428
Deferred income taxes	23,223	3,722
Total current liabilities	1,738,547	1,509,902
Long-term obligations	2,771,336	2,617,891
Deferred income taxes	647,070	656,996
Other liabilities	225,399	229,149
Commitments and contingencies		
Shareholders' equity:		
Preferred stock, 1,000 shares authorized	—	—
Common stock; $0.875 par value, 1,000,000 shares authorized, 327,069 and 338,089 shares issued and outstanding at February 1, 2013 and February 3, 2012, respectively	286,185	295,828
Additional paid-in capital	2,991,351	2,967,027
Retained earnings	1,710,732	1,416,918
Accumulated other comprehensive loss	(2,938)	(5,191)
Total shareholders' equity	4,985,330	4,674,582
Total liabilities and shareholders' equity	$ 10,367,682	$ 9,688,520

http://yahoo.brand.edgar-online.com/displayfilinginfo.aspx?FilingID=9181907-221510-451460&type=sect&dcn=0001047469-13-003283

DOLLAR GENERAL CORPORATION AND SUBSIDIARIES

CONSOLIDATED STATEMENTS OF CASH FLOWS

(In thousands)

	For the Year Ended		
	February 1, 2013	February 3, 2012	January 28, 2011
Cash flows from operating activities:			
Net income	$ 952,662	$ 766,685	$ 627,857
Adjustments to reconcile net income to net cash from operating activities:			
Depreciation and amortization	302,911	275,408	254,927
Deferred income taxes	(2,605)	10,232	50,985
Tax benefit of stock options	(87,752)	(33,102)	(13,905)
Loss on debt retirement, net	30,620	60,303	14,576
Noncash share-based compensation	21,664	15,250	15,956
Other noncash gains and losses	6,774	54,190	13,549
Change in operating assets and liabilities:			
Merchandise inventories	(391,409)	(291,492)	(251,809)
Prepaid expenses and other current assets	5,553	(34,554)	(10,157)
Accounts payable	194,035	104,442	123,424
Accrued expenses and other liabilities	(36,741)	71,763	(42,428)
Income taxes	138,711	51,550	42,903
Other	(3,071)	(195)	(1,194)
Net cash provided by (used in) operating activities	1,131,352	1,050,480	824,684
Cash flows from investing activities:			
Purchases of property and equipment	(571,596)	(514,861)	(420,395)
Proceeds from sales of property and equipment	1,760	1,026	1,448
Net cash provided by (used in) investing activities	(569,836)	(513,835)	(418,947)
Cash flows from financing activities:			
Issuance of long-term obligations	500,000	—	—
Repayments of long-term obligations	(478,255)	(911,951)	(131,180)
Borrowings under revolving credit facility	2,286,700	1,157,800	—
Repayments of borrowings under revolving credit facility	(2,184,900)	(973,100)	—
Debt issuance costs	(15,278)	—	—
Repurchases of common stock	(671,459)	(186,597)	—
Other equity transactions, net of employee taxes paid	(71,393)	(27,219)	(13,092)
Tax benefit of stock options	87,752	33,102	13,905
Net cash provided by (used in) financing activities	(546,833)	(907,965)	(130,367)
Net increase (decrease) in cash and cash equivalents	14,683	(371,320)	275,370
Cash and cash equivalents, beginning of year	126,126	497,446	222,076
Cash and cash equivalents, end of year	$ 140,809	$ 126,126	$ 497,446
Supplemental cash flow information:			
Cash paid for:			
Interest	$ 121,712	$ 209,351	$ 244,752
Income taxes	422,333	382,294	314,123
Supplemental schedule of noncash investing and financing activities:			
Purchases of property and equipment awaiting processing for payment, included in Accounts payable	$ 39,147	$ 35,662	$ 29,658
Purchases of property and equipment under capital lease obligations	$ 3,440	$ —	$ —

FAMILY DOLLAR STORES, INC., AND SUBSIDIARIES
CONSOLIDATED STATEMENTS OF INCOME

	Years Ended		
(in thousands, except per share amounts)	August 25, 2012	August 27, 2011	August 28, 2010
Net sales	$ 9,331,005	$ 8,547,835	$ 7,866,971
Cost and expenses:			
Cost of sales	6,071,058	5,515,540	5,058,971
Selling, general and administrative	2,560,346	2,394,223	2,232,402
Litigation charge	11,500	—	—
Cost of sales and operating expenses	8,642,904	7,909,763	7,291,373
Operating profit	688,101	638,072	575,598
Investment income	927	1,532	1,597
Interest expense	25,090	22,446	13,337
Income before income taxes	663,938	617,158	563,858
Income taxes	241,698	228,713	205,723
Net income	$ 422,240	$ 388,445	$ 358,135
Net income per common share—basic	$ 3.61	$ 3.15	$ 2.64
Weighted average shares—basic	117,097	123,360	135,745
Net income per common share—diluted	$ 3.58	$ 3.12	$ 2.62
Weighted average shares—diluted	118,058	124,486	136,596

http://yahoo.brand.edgar-online.com/displayfilinginfo.aspx?FilingID=8872110-150655-272840&type=sect&dcn=0000034408-12-000007

FAMILY DOLLAR STORES, INC., AND SUBSIDIARIES
CONSOLIDATED BALANCE SHEETS

(in thousands, except per share and share amounts)		August 25, 2012		August 27, 2011
Assets				
Current assets:				
Cash and cash equivalents	$	92,333	$	141,405
Short-term investment securities		6,271		96,006
Restricted cash and investments		126,281		—
Merchandise inventories		1,426,163		1,154,660
Deferred income taxes		69,518		60,011
Income tax refund receivable		—		10,326
Prepayments and other current assets		47,604		71,436
Total current assets		1,768,170		1,533,844
Property and equipment, net		1,496,360		1,280,589
Investment securities		23,720		107,458
Other assets		84,815		74,314
Total assets	$	3,373,065	$	2,996,205
Liabilities and Shareholders' Equity				
Current liabilities:				
Short-term borrowings	$	15,000	$	—
Current portion of long-term debt		16,200		16,200
Accounts payable		674,202		685,063
Accrued liabilities		328,398		310,818
Income taxes		31,857		4,974
Total current liabilities		1,065,657		1,017,055
Long-term debt		516,320		532,370
Other liabilities		268,341		270,466
Deferred gain (Note 6)		156,866		—
Deferred income taxes		68,254		89,240
Commitments and contingencies (Note 11)				
Shareholders' equity (Note 13):				
Preferred stock, $1 par; authorized 500,000 shares; no shares issued and outstanding		—		—
Common stock, $.10 par; authorized 600,000,000 shares; issued 119,125,739 shares at August 25, 2012, and 147,316,232 shares at August 27, 2011, and outstanding 115,362,048 shares at August 25, 2012, and 117,353,341 shares at August 27, 2011		11,913		14,732
Capital in excess of par		259,189		274,445
Retained earnings		1,234,384		1,969,749
Accumulated other comprehensive loss		(1,841)		(6,403)
Common stock held in treasury, at cost (3,763,691 shares at August 25, 2012, and 29,962,891 shares at August 27, 2011)		(206,018)		(1,165,449)
Total shareholders' equity		1,297,627		1,087,074
Total liabilities and shareholders' equity	$	3,373,065	$	2,996,205

FAMILY DOLLAR STORES, INC., AND SUBSIDIARIES
CONSOLIDATED STATEMENTS OF CASH FLOWS

(in thousands)	Years Ended		
	August 25, 2012	August 27, 2011	August 28, 2010
Cash flows from operating activities:			
Net income	$ 422,240	$ 388,445	$ 358,135
Adjustments to reconcile net income to net cash provided by operating activities:			
Depreciation and amortization	210,748	182,455	172,037
Deferred income taxes	(24,321)	46,805	8,123
Excess tax benefits from stock-based compensation	(12,345)	(4,745)	(1,676)
Stock-based compensation	15,902	14,728	13,163
Loss on disposition of property and equipment, including impairment	11,429	9,461	7,244
Changes in operating assets and liabilities:			
Merchandise inventories	(271,503)	(126,638)	(34,225)
Prepayments and other current assets	23,838	(8,409)	200
Other assets	(2,506)	(4,888)	2,666
Accounts payable and accrued liabilities	(36,497)	37,057	61,646
Income taxes	37,209	(23,799)	25,389
Other liabilities	(4,823)	17,592	(21,163)
	369,371	528,064	591,539
Cash flows from investing activities:			
Purchases of restricted and unrestricted investment securities	(211,142)	(352,082)	(142,730)
Sales of restricted and unrestricted investment securities	334,915	415,877	46,888
Net change in restricted cash	(80,389)	—	—
Net proceeds from sale-leaseback	359,663	—	—
Capital expenditures	(603,313)	(345,268)	(212,435)
Proceeds from dispositions of property and equipment	1,955	1,055	1,329
	(198,311)	(280,418)	(306,948)
Cash flows from financing activities:			
Revolving credit facility borrowings	362,300	46,000	—
Repayment of revolving credit facility borrowings	(347,300)	(46,000)	—
Issuance of long-term debt	—	298,482	—
Payment of debt issuance costs	—	(7,811)	(651)
Repayments of long-term debt	(16,200)	—	—
Repurchases of common stock	(191,573)	(670,466)	(332,189)
Change in cash overdrafts	26,786	(47,722)	49,687
Proceeds from exercise of employee stock options	24,900	17,216	19,663
Excess tax benefits from stock-based compensation	12,345	4,745	1,676
Payment of dividends	(91,390)	(83,439)	(78,913)
	(220,132)	(488,995)	(340,727)
Net change in cash and cash equivalents	(49,072)	(241,349)	(56,136)
Cash and cash equivalents at beginning of year	141,405	382,754	438,890

Lesson 5 Exercises

5-1. Locate the most recent 10-K report filed with the SEC for The Company your instructor selects and compare the Income Statement, Balance sheet and Statement of Cash Flows with the summary reports shown at:
- http://finance.yahoo.com/
- http://www.marketwatch.com/
- http://money.cnn.com/

5-2. Read the footnotes to the financial statements for the company you selected in 6-1 above and determine the nature of long-term debt and any "Other Liabilities."

5-3. Locate the most recent 10-K report filed with the SEC for a public company that you have selected as the entity you intend to analyze throughout the rest of the course and compare the Income Statement, Balance sheet and Statement of Cash Flows with the summary reports shown at:
- http://finance.yahoo.com/
- http://www.marketwatch.com/
- http://money.cnn.com/

5-4. Read the footnotes to the financial statements for the company you selected in 6-1 above and determine the nature of long-term debt and any "Other Liabilities."

Lesson 6: Financial Ratios [Part 1]

Purpose: To show students how financial ratios are comparisons of various financial data that can lead an analyst to a decision about the financial condition of a company.

Application: Use the "ZMF" tool found at www.businessallstars.com/calculator and show the calculation of the Z-Score, M-Score and F-Score based on data entered from various financial statements. These are three measurers used to evaluate a company's (1) potential for bankruptcy; (2) probability of earnings management; and (3) financial strength.

ZMF: Z-Score; M-Score; and F-Score

Copyright © 2007, 2013 ACBA - All Rights Reserved

XL Name Dollar General Corp. (DG)   Date 1/31/13   Calc.

Account	Current Yr	Prior Yr	2 Yrs Ago						
Cash	$141	$126		Enter data for Current Fiscal Year End					
Net Accts Receivable	$0	$0			Stock Price		Shrs O/S		
Current Assets	$2677	$2275			$46.22		327.07		
Net Fixed Assets	$2089	$1795		Equity Market Cap			$15117.1754		
Total Assets	$10368	$9689	$9546						
Current Liabilities	$1739	$1510		Click on a Wght or Test to reveal a					
Long-Term Debt	$2771	$2618		description of each measure and its formula.					
Total Liabilities	$5382	$5014	Ratios	Wght	Ratios	Wght	Ratios	Test	
Common Stock	$286	$296			-4.840		0.098	1	
Retained Earnings	$1711	$1417			+(0 x .920)		0.018	1	
Net Sales (Revenue)	$16022	$14807			+(1 x .528)		0.117	1	
Cost of Goods Sold	$10937	$10109			+(0.932 x .404)		0.019	1	
Sell, Gen & Adm Exp	$3430	$3207	(0.157 x 3.30)		+(1.082 x .892)		0	0	
E.B.I.T.	$1625	$1430	+(1.545 x 0.99)		+(1.049 x .115)		0.103	1	
Net Income	$953	$767	+(2.809 x 0.60)		-(0.988 x .172)		-0.003	0	
Depreciation Expense	$303	$275	+(0.09 x 1.20)		+(1.357 x 4.679)		0.033	1	
Oper. Cash Flow	$1131	$1050	+(0.165 x 1.40)		-(1.003 x .327)		0.966	0	

Altman's Z-Score: 'Bankruptcy Predictor'	Z-Score	M-Score	F-Score
Beneish's M-Score: 'Earnings Manipulation'	4.09	3.03	6
Piotroski's F-Score: 'Value Investing'	3.00	-2.22	0 to 9

Notes:_____

_____

_____

_____

Information from

51

Dollar General Corporation (DG) - NYSE

50.99 ↓0.10(0.20%) 12:11PM EDT - Nasdaq Real Time Price

Historical Prices

Get Historical Price

Set Date Range

Start Date: Jan ∨ 30 2013   Eg. Jan 1, 2010

End Date: Jan ∨ 31 2013

◉ Daily
○ Weekly
○ Monthly
○ Dividends Only

Get Prices

First | Previous | Next | Last

Prices

Date	Open	High	Low	Close	Volume	Adj Close*
Jan 31, 2013	46.63	46.83	46.19	46.22	3,008,800	46.22
Jan 30, 2013	47.03	47.21	46.54	46.77	4,138,800	46.77

* Close price adjusted for dividends and splits.

Information from

http://yahoo.brand.edgar-online.com/displayfilinginfo.aspx?FilingID=9181907-221510-451460&type=sect&dcn=0001047469-13-003283

Shareholders' equity:		
Preferred stock, 1,000 shares authorized	—	—
Common stock; $0.875 par value, 1,000,000 shares authorized, 327,069 and 338,089 shares issued and outstanding at February 1, 2013 and February 3, 2012, respectively	286,185	295,828
Additional paid-in capital	2,991,351	2,967,027
Retained earnings	1,710,732	1,416,918
Accumulated other comprehensive loss	(2,938)	(5,191)
Total shareholders' equity	4,985,330	4,674,582
Total liabilities and shareholders' equity	$ 10,367,682	$ 9,688,520

ZMF: Z-Score; M-Score; and F-Score

XL Name Family Dollar Stores, Inc. (FDO)   Date 8/24/12   Calc.

Account	Current Yr	Prior Yr	2 Yrs Ago
Cash	$ 219	$ 141	
Net Accts Receivable	$ 69	$ 70	
Current Assets	$ 1768	$ 1534	
Net Fixed Assets	$ 1496	$ 1281	
Total Assets	$ 3373	$ 1996	$ 2968
Current Liabilities	$ 1065	$ 1017	
Long-Term Debt	$ 516	$ 532	
Total Liabilities	$ 2075	$ 1909	
Common Stock	$ 12	$ 14	
Retained Earnings	$ 1234	$ 1969	
Net Sales (Revenue)	$ 9331	$ 8547	
Cost of Goods Sold	$ 6071	$ 5516	
Sell, Gen & Adm Exp	$ 2560	$ 2394	
E.B.I.T.	$ 689	$ 639	
Net Income	$ 422	$ 388	
Depreciation Expense	$ 210	$ 182	
Oper. Cash Flow	$ 369	$ 528	

Enter data for Current Fiscal Year End

	Stock Price	Shrs O/S
	$ 62.35	115.36

Equity Market Cap $ 7192.696

Click on a Wght or Test to reveal a description of each measure and its formula.

Ratios	Wght	Ratios	Wght	Ratios	Test
		-4.840		0.211	1
		+(0.903 x .920)		0.081	1
		+(1.015 x .528)		0.185	1
		+(-0.079 x .404)		-0.026	0
(0.204 x 3.30)		+(1.092 x .892)		-0.005	0
+(2.766 x 0.99)		+(1.011 x .115)		1.795	1
+(3.466 x 0.60)		-(0.979 x .172)		-0.114	1
+(0.208 x 1.20)		+(1.412 x 4.679)		0.152	1
+(0.366 x 1.40)		-(0.643 x .327)		0.857	0

Altman's Z-Score: 'Bankruptcy Predictor'
Beneish's M-Score: 'Earnings Manipulation'
Piotroski's F-Score: 'Value Investing'

Z-Score	M-Score	F-Score
6.28	3.84	6
3.00	-2.22	0 to 9

Notes:_____
_____
_____
_____

Information for Family Dollar Stores, Inc. from
http://finance.yahoo.com/q/hp?s=FDO&a=07&b=23&c=2012&d=07&e=24&f=2012&g=d

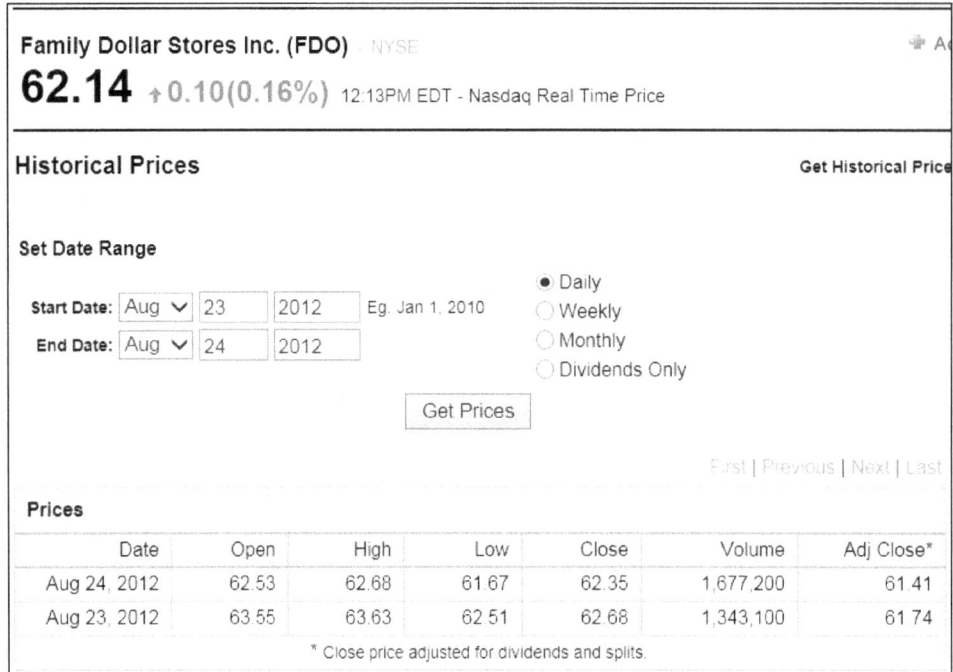

Information from
http://yahoo.brand.edgar-online.com/displayfilinginfo.aspx?FilingID=8872110-81680-
86752&type=sect&dcn=0000034408-12-000007

Shareholders' equity (Note 13):		
Preferred stock, $1 par, authorized 500,000 shares; no shares issued and outstanding	—	—
Common stock, $.10 par; authorized 600,000,000 shares; issued 119,125,739 shares at August 25, 2012, and 147,316,232 shares at August 27, 2011, and outstanding 115,362,048 shares at August 25, 2012, and 117,353,341 shares at August 27, 2011	11,913	14,732
Capital in excess of par	259,189	274,445
Retained earnings	1,234,384	1,969,749
Accumulated other comprehensive loss	(1,841)	(6,403)
Common stock held in treasury, at cost (3,763,691 shares at August 25, 2012, and 29,962,891 shares at August 27, 2011)	(206,018)	(1,165,449)
Total shareholders' equity	1,297,627	1,087,074

The Z-Score[5]

In the late 1960s, NYU professor Edward Altman published a formula to assess the probability that a firm will go bankrupt within two years. The objective was to measure financial distress along a number of objective metrics, standardizing the assessment of credit risk. He called this the Z-Score and it includes five easily derived business ratios, weighted by coefficients. Given its simplicity and accuracy, it is a common calculation used by investors and plays a relatively easy addition to an investment checklist.

Though Altman's research has been added upon in later years as new coefficients were created for more accuracy in various industries (as well as for firms in emerging markets and private firms), the original formula, widely applicable is this:

[5] http://www.frankvoisin.com/2012/05/02/what-is-the-altman-z-score/

$$Z = 1.2X_1 + 1.4X_2 + 3.3X_3 + 0.6X_4 + 0.99X_5.$$

Factor	Ratio	Objective
X_1	= Working Capital / Total Assets	Measure the liquidity of the company's asset base
X_2	= Retained Earnings / Total Assets	Measure cumulative profitability relative to firm size
X_3	= EBIT / Total Assets	Measure how efficiently the company uses its assets to generate earnings from operations
X_4	= Market Value of Equity / Book Value of Total Liabilities	Consideration of the market's view of the company relative to its liabilities
X_5	= Sales / Total Assets	Measure asset turnover

The M-Score[6]

The Beneish's M-Score looks to determine whether a company has manipulated its earnings. The M-Score has been shown to correctly identify 76% of manipulators on an out of sample basis. Here is the original M-Score formula:

$$M\text{-Score} = -4.84 + 0.92*DSRI + 0.528*GMI + 0.404*AQI + 0.892*SGI + 0.115*DEPI - 0.172*SGAI + 4.679*TATA - 0.327*LVGI$$

Factor	Name	Formula	Basis
DSRI	Days' Sales in Receivables Index	Receivables / Total Sales	This Year / Last Year
GMI	Gross Margin Index	Gross Profit / Total Sales	**Last Year / This Year**
AQI	Asset Quality Index	(Non-Current Assets – PP&E) / Total Assets	This Year / Last Year
SGI	Sales Growth Index	Total Sales	This Year / Last Year
DEPI	Depreciation Index	Depreciation / (Depreciation + Net PP&E)	**Last Year / This Year**
SGAI	SG&A Expense Index	SG&A / Revenues	This Year / Last Year
TATA	Total Accruals to Total Assets	(Working Capital – Cash) – Depreciation	This Year / Last Year
LVGI	Leverage Index	Total Debt / Total Assets	This Year / Last Year

In this original model, Beneish found that firms that scored **greater than -2.22** were more likely to be earnings manipulators.

**The Detection of Earnings Manipulation
By Messod D. Beneish**

I discuss below the measurement of each variable, and how I expect it to affect the likelihood of manipulation:

1. Days Sales in Receivables Index (DSRI):
DSRI is the ratio of days sales in receivable in the first year in which earnings manipulation is uncovered (year t) to the corresponding measure in year t-1. This variable gauges whether receivables and revenues are in or out-of-balance in two consecutive years. A large increase in day's sales in receivables could be the result of a change in credit policy to spur sales in the face of increased competition, but disproportionate increases in receivables relative to sales may also be suggestive of revenue inflation. I thus expect a large increase in days sales in receivables to be associated with a higher likelihood that revenues and earnings are overstated.

2. Gross Margin Index (GMI):
GMI is ratio of the gross margin in year t-1 to the gross margin in year t. When GMI is greater than 1, it indicates that gross margins have deteriorated. Lev and Thiagarajan (1993) suggest that gross margin deterioration is a negative signal about firms' prospects. If firms with poorer prospects are more likely to engage in earnings manipulation, I expect a positive relation between GMI and the probability of earnings manipulation.

3. Asset Quality Index (AQI):
Asset quality in a given year is the ratio of non-current assets other than property plant and equipment (PPE) to total assets and measures the proportion of total assets for which future benefits are potentially less certain. AQI is the ratio of asset quality in year t, relative to asset quality in year t-1. AQI is an aggregate measure of the change in the asset realization risk analysis suggested by Siegel (1991). If AQI is greater than 1 it indicates that the firm has potentially increased its involvement in cost deferral.9 I thus expect a positive relation between AQI and the probability of earnings manipulation. An increase in asset realization risk indicates an increased propensity to capitalize and thus defer costs.

4. Sales Growth Index (SGI):
SGI is the ratio of sales in year t to sales in year t-1. Growth does not imply manipulation, but growth firms are viewed by professionals as more likely to commit financial statement fraud because their financial position and capital needs put pressure on managers to achieve earnings targets (National Commission on Fraudulent Financial Reporting (1987), National Association of Certified Fraud Examiners (1993)). In addition, concerns about controls and reporting tend to lag behind operations in periods of high growth (National Commission on Fraudulent Financial Reporting (1987), Loebeckke et al. (1989)). If growth firms face large stock prices losses at the first indication of a slowdown, they may have greater incentives to manipulate earnings. To this effect, Fridson (1993, pp. 7-8) states: "Almost invariably, companies try to dispel the impression that their growth is decelerating, since that perception can be so costly to them." I thus expect a positive relation between SGI and the probability of earnings manipulation.

5. Depreciation Index (DEPI):
DEPI is the ratio of the rate of depreciation in year t-1 vs the corresponding rate in year t. The depreciation rate in a given year equals is equal to depreciation/(depreciation+net PPE). A DEPI greater

than 1 it indicates that the rate at which assets are depreciated has slowed down--raising the possibility that the firm has revised upwards the estimates of assets useful lives or adopted a new method that is income increasing. I thus expect a positive relation between DEPI and the probability of manipulation.

6.Sales General and Administrative Expenses Index (SGAI):
SGAI is calculated as the ratio of SGA to sales in year t relative to the corresponding measure in year t-1. The variable is used following Lev and Thiagarajan's (1993) suggestion that analysts would interpret a disproportionate increase in sales as a negative signal about firms future prospects. I expect a positive relation between SGAI and the probability of manipulation.

7. Leverage Index (LVGI):
LVGI is the ratio of total debt to total assets in year t relative to the corresponding ratio in year t-1. A LVGI greater than 1 indicates an increase in leverage. The variable is included to capture debt covenants incentives for earnings manipulation. Assuming that leverage follows a random walk, LVGI implicitly measures the leverage forecast error. I use the change in leverage in the firms' capital structure given evidence in Beneish and Press (1993) that such changes are associated with the stock market effect of default.

8. Total Accruals to Total Assets (TATA):
Total accruals are calculated as the change in working capital accounts other than cash less depreciation. Either total accruals or a partition thereof has been used in prior work to assess the extent to which managers make discretionary accounting choices to alter earnings (see for example Healy (1985), Jones (1991). I use total accruals to total assets to proxy for the extent to which cash underlies reported earnings, and expect higher positive accruals (less cash) to be associated with a higher likelihood of earnings manipulation.

http://myweb.ncku.edu.tw/~r16001205/w7.1_ProbM_Model.FAJ.1999.pdf

The F-Score[7]

The F-Score identifies the healthiest companies. Piotroski noticed that, among apparent value stocks (firms with high book-to-market ratios, or low P/B), some ultimately were strong performers while others collapsed. He sought out a method of separating out the value traps. He did so by also considering accounting ratios (as in the Z-Score), but rather than analyzing these ratios at one point in time, he placed the emphasis on the change in these ratios over time.

The Piotroski's F-Score Equation is:

$$\text{F-Score} = \text{ROA} + \Delta\text{ROA} + \text{CFO} + \text{ACCRUAL} + \Delta\text{MARGIN} + \Delta\text{TURN} + \Delta\text{LEVER} + \Delta\text{LIQUID} + \text{EQOFFER}$$

Piotroski's nine factors are split into three groups:

Factor	Ratio	Scoring
Profitability Signals		

---

[7] http://www.frankvoisin.com/2012/05/04/what-is-the-piotroski-f-score/

ROA	Net Income / Total Assets	+1 if positive this year
ΔROA	(Cur. NI / TA) / (Prior NI / TA)	+1 if positive yr. over yr.
CFO	Operating Cash Flow / Total Assets	+1 if positive this year
ACCRUAL	Operating Cash Flow / Net Income	+1 if positive this year
Operating Efficiency Signals		
ΔMARGIN	Cur. Gross Margin / Prior Gross Margin	+1 if increase yr. over yr.
ΔTURN	(Cur. Sales / TA) / (Prior Sales / TA)	+1 if increase yr. over yr.
Leverage, Liquidity and Source of Funds Signals		
ΔLEVER	(Cur. Debt / TA) / (Prior Debt / TA)	+1 if decrease yr. over yr.
ΔLIQUID	(Cur. CA / CL) / (Prior CA / CL)	+1 if increase yr. over yr.
EQOFFER	Cur. Com Stock – Prior Com Stock	+1 if no change

"Value Investing: The Use of Historical Financial Statement Information to Separate Winners from Losers"
By Joseph D. Piotroski
The University of Chicago
Graduate School of Business

I use four variables to measure these performance-related factors: ROA, CFO, ▲ROA, and ACCRUAL. I define ROA and CFO as net income before extraordinary items and cash flow from operations, respectively, scaled by beginning of the year total assets. If the firm's ROA (CFO) is positive, I define the indicator variable F_ROA (F_CFO) equal to one, zero otherwise. I define ▲ROA as the current year's ROA less the prior year's ROA. If ▲ROA>0, the indicator variable F_▲ROA equals one, zero otherwise.

The relationship between earnings and cash flow levels is also considered. Sloan (1996) shows that earnings driven by positive accrual adjustments (i.e., profits are greater than cash flow from operations) is a bad signal about future profitability and returns. This relationship may be particularly important among value firms, where the incentive to manage earnings through positive accruals (e.g., to prevent covenant violations) is strong (e.g., Sweeney 1994). I define the variable ACCRUAL as current year's net income before extraordinary items less cash flow from operations, scaled by beginning of the year total assets. The indicator variable F_ACCRUAL equals one if CFO >ROA, zero otherwise.

2.3.2 Financial performance signals: Leverage, liquidity, and source of funds
Three of the nine financial signals are designed to measure changes in capital structure and the firm's ability to meet future debt service obligations: ▲LEVER, ▲LIQUID, and EQ_OFFER. Since most high BM firms are financially constrained, I assume that an increase in leverage, a deterioration of liquidity, or the use of external financing is a bad signal about financial risk.

▲LEVER as the historical change in the ratio of total long-term debt to average total assets, and view an increase (decrease) in financial leverage as a negative (positive) signal. By raising external capital, a financially distressed firm is signaling its inability to generate sufficient internal funds (e.g., Myers and Majluf 1984, Miller and Rock 1985). In addition, an increase in long-term debt is likely to place additional constraints on the firm's financial flexibility. I define the indicator variable F_▲LEVER to equal one (zero) if the firm's leverage ratio fell (rose) in the year preceding portfolio formation.

The variable ▲LIQUID measures the historical change in the firm's current ratio between the current and prior year, where I define the current ratio as the ratio of current assets to current liabilities at fiscal year-end. I assume that an improvement in liquidity (i.e., ▲LIQUID>0) is a good signal about the firm's ability to service current debt obligations. The indicator variable F_▲LIQUID equals one if the firm's liquidity improved, zero otherwise.

I define the indicator variable EQ_OFFER to equal one if the firm did not issue common equity in the year preceding portfolio formation, zero otherwise. Similar to an increase in long-term debt, financially distressed firms that raise external capital could be signaling their inability to generate sufficient internal funds to service future obligations (e.g., Myers and Majluf 1984; Miller and Rock 1985). Moreover, the fact that these firms are willing to issue equity when their stock prices are likely to be depressed (i.e., high cost of capital) highlights the poor financial condition facing these firms.

2.3.3 Financial performance signals: Operating efficiency
The remaining two signals are designed to measure changes in the efficiency of the firm's operations: ▲MARGIN and ▲TURN. These ratios are important because they reflect two key constructs underlying a decomposition of return on assets.

I define ▲MARGIN as the firm's current gross margin ratio (gross margin scaled by total sales) less the prior year's gross margin ratio. An improvement in margins signifies a potential improvement in factor costs, a reduction in inventory costs, or a rise in the price of the firm's product. The indicator variable F_▲MARGIN equals one if ▲MARGIN is positive, zero otherwise.

I define ▲TURN as the firm's current year asset turnover ratio (total sales scaled by beginning of the year total assets) less the prior year's asset turnover ratio. An improvement in asset turnover signifies greater productivity from the asset base. Such an improvement can arise from more efficient operations (fewer assets generating the same levels of sales) or an increase in sales (which could also signify improved market conditions for the firm's products). The indicator variable F_▲TURN equals one if ▲TURN is positive, zero otherwise.

2.3.4 Composite score
As indicated earlier, I define F_SCORE as the sum of the individual binary signals, or

$$F\_SCORE = F\_ROA\_F\_▲ROA\_F\_CFO\_F\_ACCRUAL\_F\_▲MARGIN$$
$$\_F\_▲TURN\_F\_▲LEVER\_F\_▲LIQUID\_EQ\_OFFER.$$

Given the nine underlying signals, F_SCORE can range from a low of 0 to a high of 9, where a low (high) F_SCORE represents a firm with very few (mostly) good signals. To the extent current fundamentals predict future fundamentals, I expect F_SCORE to be positively associated with changes in future firm performance and stock returns.

http://www.chicagobooth.edu/~/media/FE874EE65F624AAEBD0166B1974FD74D.pdf

Lesson 6 Exercises

6-1. Complete a ZMF model for The Company your instructor selects making sure the price per share and the number of shares outstanding are as of the most recent fiscal year end consistent with the financial data entered into the form.

6-2. Complete a ZMF model for a public company that you have selected as the entity you intend to analyze throughout the rest of this course. Make sure the price per share and the number of shares outstanding is as of the most recent fiscal year end consistent with the financial data entered into the form.

6-3. Select ten companies that are publicly traded. Calculate their Z-score, M-score, and F-Score. Then calculate their current imbedded interest rate (interest expense divided by interest-bearing debt). Record the results of your calculations in the table below. If you are part of a class, the class may be divided up into ten teams to analyze one company each.

Company	Z-Score	M-Score	F-Score	Interest Rate

- Does there appear to be any consistency between the various scores? In other words do companies with low Z-scores also have low M-scores and low F-scores?
- Does the interest rate for each company reflect the risk associated with the various scores? Do low interest rates coincide with high scores and higher rates with low scores?
- What if any, is the general conclusion that can be reached from this analysis?

6-4. Create a computer spreadsheet that will emulate the ZMF model with data for the company in 7-1 above.

Lesson 7: Financial Ratios [Part 2]

Purpose: To show students how financial ratios are comparisons of various financial data that can lead an analyst to a decision about the financial condition of a company.

Application: The www.businessallstars.com/calculator site has analytical tools for examining a company's relative performance against itself, other companies or over time. Use the "roi," "comp," and "nwc" tools to generate critical comparisons that senior management may use to tell if a company is operating at peak performance. These are all classic measures that most companies have used for years.

ROI-Return On Investment (ROA & ROE)
Copyright © 2013 ACBA - All Rights Reserved
BusinessAllstars.com

XL   Name Dollar General Corp (DG)   Date 1/31/13

Input		Output		Results	
Total Revenue (Rev) $ 16022					
Net Income (NI) $ 953		**Profit Margin (PM)**	NI / TR	5.95	%
Dividends Paid (DP) $ 0		**Payout Ratio (PR)**	DP / NI	0	%
		Retention Ratio (RR)	1 - PR	100	%
Total Assets (TA) $ 10368		**Total Asset Turnover (TAT)**	Rev / TA	1.55	x
Common Equity (CE) $ 4985		**Equity Multiplier (EM)**	TA / CE	2.08	x
		Return on Assets (ROA)	PM x TAT	9.22	%
		Return on Equity (ROE)	ROA x EM	19.18	%
		Internal Growth Rate	$\frac{(ROA \times RR)}{(1 - ROA \times RR)}$	10.16	%
Calc.		**Sustainable Growth Rate**	$\frac{(ROE \times RR)}{(1 - ROE \times RR)}$	23.73	%

"My Year with General Motors" By Alfred P. Sloan:

"When Donaldson Brown came to General Motors he brought with him a financial yardstick. It was a method of crystallizing facts bearing on the efficiency of management in the various phases of the business, such as inventory control, plans for capital investment in relation to expected demands on production, cost control, and the like. In other words, Mr. Brown developed the concept of return on investment in such a way that it could be used to measure the effectiveness of each division's operation as well as to evaluate broad investment decisions. His concept can be expressed in the form of an equation for computing return on investment, and it is still one of the measures used by the du Pont Company and General Motors to evaluate division performance."

"Rate of return, of course, is affected by all the factors in the business; hence if one can see how these factors individually bear upon a rate of return, one has a penetrating look into the business. To obtain this insight, Mr. Brown defined return on investment as a function of the profit margin and the rate of turnover of invested capital.[8]"

---

[8] Sloan, Alfred P., "My Years with General Motors," Doubleday, New York, 1963, Page 141

ROI-Return On Investment (ROA & ROE)

XL Name | Family Dollar Stores, Inc. (FDO) | Date | 8/24/12 |

Input			Output		Results	
Total Revenue (Rev)	$ 9331					
Net Income (NI)	$ 422		**Profit Margin (PM)**	NI / TR	4.52	%
Dividends Paid (DP)	$ 91		**Payout Ratio (PR)**	DP / NI	21.56	%
			Retention Ratio (RR)	1 - PR	78.44	%
Total Assets (TA)	$ 3373		**Total Asset Turnover (TAT)**	Rev / TA	2.77	x
Common Equity (CE)	$ 1298		**Equity Multiplier (EM)**	TA / CE	2.6	x
			Return on Assets (ROA)	PM x TAT	12.52	%
			Return on Equity (ROE)	ROA x EM	32.55	%
			Internal Growth Rate	$\frac{(ROA \times RR)}{(1 - ROA \times RR)}$	10.89	%
Calc.			**Sustainable Growth Rate**	$\frac{(ROE \times RR)}{(1 - ROE \times RR)}$	34.29	%

Notes:_____

_____

_____

_____

62

There are a myriad of ratios that can be calculated. Some of the most basic are found in most college text books. By referring to the http://www.reuters.com/finance/stocks web site a great set of comparisons can be found. Enter the data from that site for the respective companies in the cells provided and see the "Total Score" in the bottom right hand corner.

COMP - Comp Ratio Analysis		Name	Dollar General Corp (DG)		Date	6/6/2013			
			www.businessallstars.com						
	Company	Industry				Company	Industry		
P/E Ratio (TTM)	17.33	27.05	-1	Interest Coverage (TTM)		9.15	20.56	-1	
P/E High - Last 5 Yrs.	22.48	28.68	-1	Gross Margin (TTM)		31.5	22.46	1	
P/E Low - Last 5 Yrs.	15.6	15.58	1	Gross Margin - 5 Yr. Avg.		31.32	21.51	1	
Beta	0.14	0.79	1	EBITD Margin (TTM)		12.39	0		
Price to Sales (TTM)	1	1.16	-1	EBITD - 5 Yr. Avg		11.41	7.65	1	
Price to Book (MRQ)	3.17	5.5	-1	Operating Margin (TTM)		10.19	6.4	1	
Price to Tangible Book (MRQ)	0	6.6		Operating Margin - 5 Yr. Avg.		9	5.75	1	
Price to Cash Flow (TTM)	12.93	18.82	-1	Pre-Tax Margin (TTM)		9.19	6.43	1	
Price to Free Cash Flow (TTM)	32.18	37.81	-1	Pre-Tax Margin - 5 Yr. Avg.		6.74	5.78	1	
Dividend Yield	0	1.2		Net Profit Margin (TTM)		5.87	4.42	1	
Dividend Yield - 5 Year Avg.	0	1.4		Net Profit Margin - 5 Yr. Avg.		4.23	4.01	1	
Dividend 5 Year Growth Rate	0	19.12		Effective Tax Rate (TTM)		36.19	31.4	-1	
Payout Ratio(TTM)	0	34.35		Effecitve Tax Rate - 5 Yr. Avg.		37.25	30.74	-1	
Sales (MRQ) vs Qtr. 1 Yr. Ago	8.5	6.37	1	Revenue/Employee (TTM)		180,714	########	-1	
Sales (TTM) vs TTM 1 Yr. Ago	7.2	8.11	-1	Net Income/Employee (TTM)		10,600	1,574,258	-1	
Sales - 5 Yr. Growth Rate	11.03	12.07	-1	Receivable Turnover (TTM)		0	154.95		
EPS (MRQ) vs Qtr. 1 Yr. Ago	6.69	-45.79	1	Inventory Turnover (TTM)		5.07	8.24	-1	
EPS (TTM) vs TTM 1 Yr. Ago	20.82	0		Asset Turnover (TTM)		1.61	2.05	-1	
EPS - 5 Yr. Growth Rate	0	12.02		Return on Assets (TTM)		9.47	8.88	1	
Cap Spending - 5 Yr. Growth Rate	32.53	5.73	1	Return on Assets - 5 Yr. Avg.		6.01	8.27	-1	
Quick Ratio (MRQ)	0.19	0.52	-1	Return on Investment (TTM)		11.12	15.28	-1	
Current Ratio (MRQ)	1.7	1.08	1	Return on Investment - 5 Yr. Avg.		6.98	13.26	-1	
LT Debt to Equity (MRQ)	54.75	25.97	-1	Return on Equity (TTM)		19.64	19.23	1	
Total Debt to Equity (MRQ)	54.76	41.85	-1	Return on Equity - 5 Yr. Avg.		14.87	16.72	-1	
							Total Score:	-5	

Company > Industry
Industry > Company
Company > 1

Notes:_____
_____
_____
_____

| COMP - Comp Ratio Analysis | Name | Family Dollar Stores, Inc. (FDO) | | | Date | 6/6/2013 |

www.businessallstars.com

	Company	Industry			Company	Industry	
P/E Ratio (TTM)	16.43	27.05	-1	Interest Coverage (TTM)	25.13	20.56	1
P/E High - Last 5 Yrs.	17.43	28.68	-1	Gross Margin (TTM)	34.25	22.46	1
P/E Low - Last 5 Yrs.	14.8	15.58	-1	Gross Margin - 5 Yr. Avg.	34.95	21.51	1
Beta	0.13	0.79	1	EBITD Margin (TTM)	9.11	0	
Price to Sales (TTM)	0.69	1.16	-1	EBITD - 5 Yr. Avg	8.97	7.65	1
Price to Book (MRQ)	4.84	5.5	-1	Operating Margin (TTM)	6.73	6.4	1
Price to Tangible Book (MRQ)	4.84	6.6	-1	Operating Margin - 5 Yr. Avg.	6.79	5.75	1
Price to Cash Flow (TTM)	10.56	18.82	-1	Pre-Tax Margin (TTM)	6.62	6.43	1
Price to Free Cash Flow (TTM)		37.81		Pre-Tax Margin - 5 Yr. Avg.	6.62	5.78	1
Dividend Yield	1.74	1.2	1	Net Profit Margin (TTM)	4.24	4.42	-1
Dividend Yield - 5 Year Avg.	1.4	1.4	-1	Net Profit Margin - 5 Yr. Avg.	4.22	4.01	1
Dividend 5 Year Growth Rate	5.92	19.12	-1	Effective Tax Rate (TTM)	35.92	31.4	-1
Payout Ratio(TTM)	17.14	34.35	-1	Effecitve Tax Rate - 5 Yr. Avg.	36.29	30.74	-1
Sales (MRQ) vs Qtr. 1 Yr. Ago	17.71	6.37	1	Revenue/Employee (TTM)	304,235	########	-1
Sales (TTM) vs TTM 1 Yr. Ago	12.87	8.11	1	Net Income/Employee (TTM)	12,906	1,574,258	-1
Sales - 5 Yr. Growth Rate	6.43	12.07	-1	Receivable Turnover (TTM)	761.63	154.95	1
EPS (MRQ) vs Qtr. 1 Yr. Ago	4.84	-45.79	1	Inventory Turnover (TTM)	4.79	8.24	-1
EPS (TTM) vs TTM 1 Yr. Ago	7.33	0		Asset Turnover (TTM)	2.92	2.05	1
EPS - 5 Yr. Growth Rate	17.11	12.02	1	Return on Assets (TTM)	12.39	8.88	1
Cap Spending - 5 Yr. Growth Rate	35.6	5.73	1	Return on Assets - 5 Yr. Avg.	11.67	8.27	1
Quick Ratio (MRQ)	0.33	0.52	-1	Return on Investment (TTM)	18.58	15.28	1
Current Ratio (MRQ)	1.52	1.08	1	Return on Investment - 5 Yr. Avg.	18	13.26	1
LT Debt to Equity (MRQ)	35.11	25.97	-1	Return on Equity (TTM)	32.2	19.23	1
Total Debt to Equity (MRQ)	49.04	41.85	-1	Return on Equity - 5 Yr. Avg.	26.3	16.72	1
					Total Score:	**5**	

Company > Industry
Industry > Company
Company > 1

Notes:_____
_____
_____
_____

Probably the single most critical set of ratios that can be calculated are those dealing with working capital. These involve looking at a company's cash, accounts receivable, inventory, and accounts payable levels. Often working capital is translated into how many days are tied up in each of these areas. Some companies maintain excess cash that is often considered non-operating.

NWC-Net Working Capital Analysis
Copyright © 2013 ACBA - All Rights Reserved
BusinessAllstars.com

XL   Name Dollar General Stores, Inc (DG)   Date 1/31/13   Calc.

Description	Last Year	1 Year Ago	2 Years Ago		Net DAYS	External Funding
Accts Rec	0	0	0	1st Yr	21.99	659
Inventory	2397	2009	1765	2nd Yr	18.05	500
Accts Pay	1738	1509	1364	3rd Yr	16.52	401
Revenue	16022	14807	13035	Average	19	520
Cost of Rev	10937	10109	8858			
A/R Days	0 days	0 days	0 days			
Inv Days	79.99 days	72.54 days	72.73 days			
A/P Days	58 days	54.48 days	56.2 days			

					Non-Oper
Cash+Eqiv	141	126	497	1st Yr Excess	-179
S-Term Inv	0	0	0	2nd Yr Excess	-170
Total	141	126	497	3rd Yr Excess	236
Limit (2% rev)	320	296	261	Average Excess	-38

Notes:_____
_____
_____
_____

NWC-Net Working Capital Analysis
Copyright © 2013 ACBA - All Rights Reserved
BusinessAllstars.com

XL Name: Family Dollar Stores, Inc. (FDO)   Date: 8/24/12   Calc.

Description	Last Year	1 Year Ago	2 Years Ago		Net DAYS	External Funding
Accts Rec	70	70	52	1st Yr	26.31	438
Inventory	1426	1155	1028	2nd Yr	13.19	199
Accts Pay	1034	1001	1005	3rd Yr	4.07	56
Revenue	9331	8528	7867	Average	15	231
Cost of Rev	6071	5516	5059			
A/R Days	2.74 days	3 days	2.41 days			
Inv Days	85.73 days	76.43 days	74.17 days			
A/P Days	62.17 days	66.24 days	72.51 days			

						Non-Oper
Cash+Eqiv	219	141	383	1st Yr Excess		38
S-Term Inv	6	96	120	2nd Yr Excess		66
Total	225	237	503	3rd Yr Excess		346
Limit (2% rev)	187	171	157	Average Excess		150

"Managing" by Harold Geneen:

"The ability to pay or to refinance your debts as they come due is absolutely essential. The only irreparable mistake in business is to run out of cash. Almost any other mistake in business can be remedied in one way or another. But when you run out of cash, they take you out of the game.[9]"

Lesson 7 Exercises

7-1. Complete the ROI, Comp, and NWC models for the company your instructor selects for the most recent fiscal year end.

7-2 Complete the ROI, Comp, and NWC models for the company you have selected for analysis during this course.

---

[9] Geneen, Harold, "Managing," Doubleday, New York, 1984, Page 192

Lesson 8: Cost of Debt and Bond Ratings

Purpose: Introduce students to long-term financing by the use of bonds, how they are rated by agencies and how interest rates are set by those agencies for the market place.

Application: Use the "rate" and "bond" tools at www.businessallstars.com/calculator to first find the bond rating that would apply to a specific company and then based on that rating find what the current Yield-to-Maturity (YTM) would be. These tools are not exactly what a rating agency would use, but they are close estimates. Agencies use more tools than just a ratio based calculation.

Rate-Determining a Bond Rating

Name — Dollar General Corp. (DG) Date 01/31/13

	Account	End Yr	Beg Yr	Calculations	Ratios	Rating	#
1	Sales	16,022		EBIT / Int Exp	12.70	A	
2	EBIT (Net Operating Income)	1,625		EBITDA / Int Exp	15.06	A	
3	Interest Expense	128		(NI + DE) / TD	23.3%	BB	
4	Net Income (cont oper) [NI]	953		(CF - CE) / TD	10.4%	BB	
5	Depreciation Expense [DE]	303		EBIT / avg (TD + SE)	19.1%	A	
6	Cashflow from Operations (CF)	1,131		EBITDA / Sales	12.0%	CCC	
7	Capital Expenditures (CE)	572		LTD / (LTD + SE)	35.7%	BBB	
8	Long-Term Debt [LTD]	2,771		TD / (TD + SE)	51.9%	BB	
9	Total Debt [TD]	5,382	5,014				
10	Stockholder's Equity [SE]	4,985	1,675	Approximate Bond Rating		BBB	

Rate-Determining a Bond Rating

Name — Family Dollar Stores, Inc (FDO) Date 08/24/12

	Account	End Yr	Beg Yr	Calculations	Ratios	Rating	#
1	Sales	9,331		EBIT / Int Exp	27.56	AAA	
2	EBIT (Net Operating Income)	689		EBITDA / Int Exp	36.00	AAA	
3	Interest Expense	25		(NI + DE) / TD	30.5%	BB	
4	Net Income (cont oper) [NI]	422		(CF - CE) / TD	-11.3%	CC	
5	Depreciation Expense [DE]	211		EBIT / avg (TD + SE)	21.6%	A	
6	Cashflow from Operations (CF)	369		EBITDA / Sales	9.6%	CCC	
7	Capital Expenditures (CE)	603		LTD / (LTD + SE)	28.4%	A	
8	Long-Term Debt [LTD]	516		TD / (TD + SE)	61.5%	B	
9	Total Debt [TD]	2,075	1,909				
10	Stockholder's Equity [SE]	1,298	1,087	Approximate Bond Rating		BBB	

Notes:_____

_____

_____

_____

The bond tool is uses a random selection of "B" rated bonds to find the average they are currently paying as their YTM. The user will also find the current "AAA" corporate bond rating and from these two a profile will be developed to show what the rate would be for bonds rated from "AAA" down to "CC." Long-term ratings are used as opposed to short-term because of the great fluctuation that can occur in the near term. Usually, somewhere between 10 to 20 years is generally used.

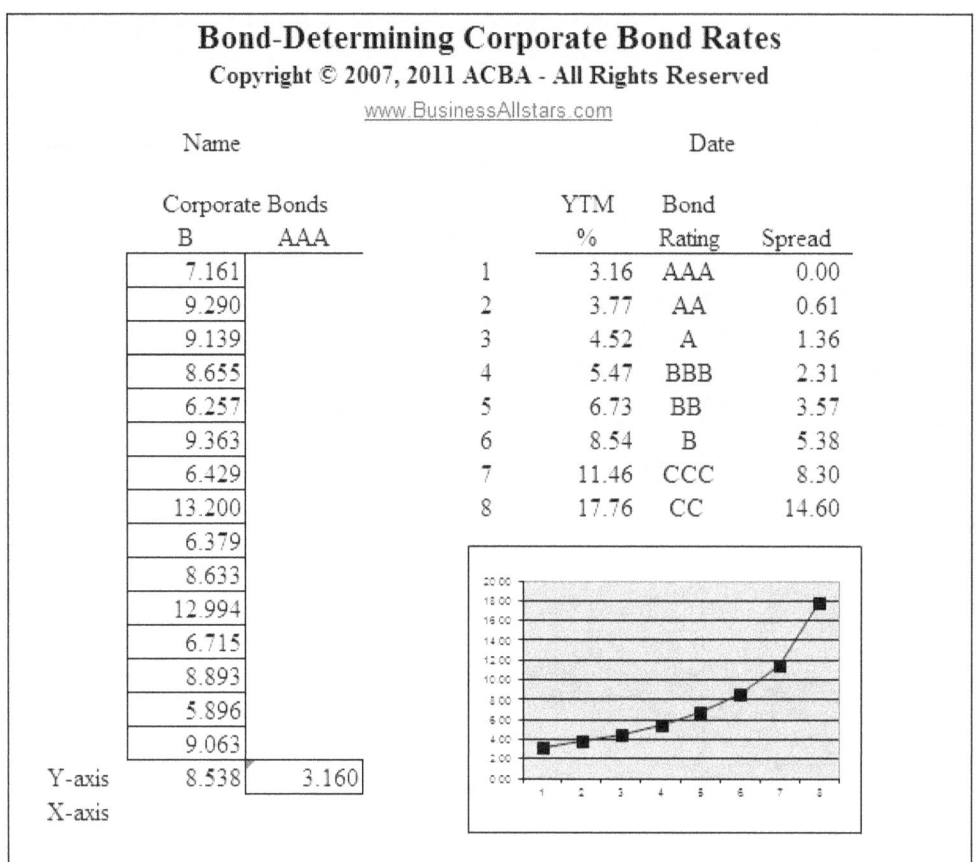

Bond-Determining Corporate Bond Rates
Copyright © 2007, 2011 ACBA - All Rights Reserved
www.BusinessAllstars.com

	Name				Date	
	Corporate Bonds			YTM	Bond	
	B	AAA		%	Rating	Spread
	7.161		1	3.16	AAA	0.00
	9.290		2	3.77	AA	0.61
	9.139		3	4.52	A	1.36
	8.655		4	5.47	BBB	2.31
	6.257		5	6.73	BB	3.57
	9.363		6	8.54	B	5.38
	6.429		7	11.46	CCC	8.30
	13.200		8	17.76	CC	14.60
	6.379					
	8.633					
	12.994					
	6.715					
	8.893					
	5.896					
	9.063					
Y-axis	8.538	3.160				
X-axis						

A good place to find the data that is needed in at http://finance.yahoo.com/bonds.

Lesson 8 Exercises

8-1. Complete a Rate and Bond models for The company your instructor selects making sure the price per share and the number of shares outstanding are as of the most recent fiscal year end consistent with the financial data entered into the form.

8-2. Complete a Rate and Bond models for a public company that you have selected as the entity you intend to analyze throughout the rest of this course. Make sure the price per share and the number of shares outstanding is as of the most recent fiscal year end consistent with the financial data entered into the form.

Lesson 9: Invested Capital

Purpose: Show students how accounting financial statements can be converted to data that is usable for analytical purposes. Introduce the students to "Invested Capital" and "NOPAT."

Application: Use the 'ICE' tool found at www.businessallstars.com/calculator to find the Invested Capital for a company. It will show the Operating Approach (Book Value) and balance that with the Financing Approach (Book Value). It will also show how the Financing Approach (Market Value) can be calculated. Each of these is useful for various different purposes.

ICE®-Invested Capital Equality
Copyright © 2013 ACBA - All Rights Reserved
BusinessAllstars.com

XL **Name** Dollar General Corp. (DG)   **Date** 1/31/13   Calc.

1-Operating Approach (BV)	Current Yr End	3-Financing Approach (MV)	Current Yr End	% Cap Str	
Current Assets	$ 2677	Total Interest-bearing Debt	$ 2772	15.5	%
Revenue $ 16022		Preferred Equity	$ 0	0	%
Cash Equivalents $ 141	$ -179.44	Market Capitalization of Equity $ 15117		84.5	%
Net Operating Current Assets	$ 2856.44	**Invested Capital (MV)**	$ 17889	100	%
Current Liabilities	$ 1739				
Less: Interest-Bearing Debt	$ 1	2-Financing Approach (BV)	Current Yr End	% Cap Str	
Net Operating Current Liabilities	$ 1738	Interest-Bearing Debt (Current)	$ 1		
Net Operating Working Capital	$ 1118.44	Long-term Debt	$ 2771		
		Total Interest-bearing Debt	$ 2772	35.74	%
Total Assets	$ 10368				
Less: Current Assets	$ 2677	Stockholder's Equity (BV)	$ 4985		
Net Long-term Assets	$ 7691	Preferred Equity (BV)	$ 0	0	%
Plus: Net Oper. Working Capital	$ 1118.44	Common Equity (BV)	$ 4985	64.26	%
Less: Long-term Non-Oper	$ 1052.440000000				
Invested Capital (BV))	$ 7757	**Invested Capital (BV)**	$ 7757	100	%
Non-Operating Assets	$ 873.0000000000	MV/BV of Equity	3.03	%	

ZMF: Z-Score; M-Score; and F-Score
Copyright © 2007, 2013 ACBA - All Rights Reserved

XL Name Dollar General Corp. (DG)   Date 1/31/13   Calc.

Account	Current Yr	Prior Yr	2 Yrs Ago		
Cash	$ 141	$ 126		Enter data for Current Fiscal Year End	
Net Accts Receivable	$ 0	$ 0		Stock Price	Shrs O/S
Current Assets	$ 2677	$ 2275		$ 46.22	327.07
Net Fixed Assets	$ 2089	$ 1795		Equity Market Cap	$ 15117.1754
Total Assets	$ 10368	$ 9620	$ 9546		

ICE®-Invested Capital Equality

XL Name Family Dollar Stores Inc. (FDO)   **Date** 8/24/12   **Calc.**

1-Operating Approach (BV)		Current Yr End	3-Financing Approach (MV)	Current Yr End	% Cap Str	
Current Assets		$ 1768	Total Interest-bearing Debt	$ 516	6.69	%
Revenue	$ 9331		Preferred Equity	$ 0	0	%
Cash Equivalents $ 224		$ 37.37999999999	Market Capitalization of Equity	$ 7192.7	93.31	%
Net Operating Current Assets		$ 1730.62	**Invested Capital (MV)**	$ 7708.7	100	%
Current Liabilities		$ 1066				
Less: Interest-Bearing Debt		$ 0	2-Financing Approach (BV)	Current Yr End	% Cap Str	
Net Operating Current Liabilities		$ 1066	Interest-Bearing Debt (Current)	$ 0		
Net Operating Working Capital		$ 664.6199999999	Long-term Debt	$ 516		
			Total Interest-bearing Debt	$ 516	28.45	%
Total Assets		$ 3373				
Less: Current Assets		$ 1768	Stockholder's Equity (BV)	$ 1298		
Net Long-term Assets		$ 1605	Preferred Equity (BV)	$ 0	0	%
Plus: Net Oper. Working Capital		$ 664.6199999999	Common Equity (BV)	$ 1298	71.55	%
Less: Long-term Non-Oper		$ 455.6199999999				
Invested Capital (BV))		$ 1814	**Invested Capital (BV)**	$ 1814	100	%
Non-Operating Assets		$ 492.9999999999	MV/BV of Equity		5.54	%

ZMF: Z-Score; M-Score; and F-Score

XL Name Family Dollar Stores, Inc. (FDO)   **Date** 8/24/12   **Calc.**

Account	Current Yr	Prior Yr	2 Yrs Ago		
Cash	$ 219	$ 141		Enter data for Current Fiscal Year End	
Net Accts Receivable	$ 69	$ 70		Stock Price	Shrs O/S
Current Assets	$ 1768	$ 1534		$ 62.35	115.36
Net Fixed Assets	$ 1496	$ 1281		Equity Market Cap	$ 7192.696
Total Assets	$ 3373	$ 1006	$ 2968		

"**Invested capital** represents the total cash investment that shareholders and debtholders have made in a company. There are two different but completely equivalent methods for calculating invested capital.

The *operating approach* is calculated as:

Invested capital = operating net working capital + net property, plant & equipment + capitalized operating leases + other operating assets + operating intangibles − other operating liabilities − cumulative adjustment for amortization of R&D.

Equivalently, the *financing approach* is calculated as:

70

> Invested Capital = total debt and leases + total equity and equity equivalents – non operating cash and investments.
>
> Invested capital is used in several important measurements of financial performance, including return on invested capital, economic value added, and free cash flow.[10&11]"

Many texts refer to Invested Capital by various names

Ehrhardt and Brigham: "In addition to working capital, most companies also use long-term assets to support their operations. These include land, buildings, factories, equipment, and the like. Total net operating capital is the sum of NOWC and operating long-term assets.[12]" Then they say: "One way to determine whether growth is profitable is by examining the return on invested capital (ROIC), which is the ratio of NOPAT to total operating capital.[13]" They seem to use three terms for the same concept (1) Total net operating capital; (2) Invested Capital; and (3) total operating capital.

Easton, Halsey, McAnally, Hartgraves: "Net Operating Assets (NOA): Current and long-term operating assets less current and long-term operating liabilities; or net operating working capital plus long-term operating assets.[14]" Earlier in the text they refer to Return on Investment and say: "The return on investment of an investment center is computed by dividing the income of the center by its asset base (usually total assets): ROI = (Investment center in come / Investment center asset base).[15]"

Lesson 9 Exercises

9-1. Complete a ICE model for The company your instructor selects making sure the price per share and the number of shares outstanding are as of the most recent fiscal year end consistent with the financial data entered into the form.

9-2. Complete a ICE model for a public company that you have selected as the entity you intend to analyze throughout the rest of this course. Make sure the price per share and the number of shares outstanding is as of the most recent fiscal year end consistent with the financial data entered into the form.

---

[10] Brealey, Myers, and Allen. *Principles of Corporate Finance*, 8th edition (McGraw-Hill/Irwin, 2005).

[11] G. Bennett Stewart III. *The Quest for Value* (HarperCollins, 1991).

[12] Ehrhardt, Brigham, *Corporate Finance: A focused Approach*, (SouthWestern, 4th ed. 2011), page 61

[13] Ehrhardt, Brigham, *Corporate Finance: A focused Approach*, (SouthWestern, 4th ed. 2011), page 66

[14] Easton, Halsey, McAnally, Hartgraves, Morse, Financial & Managerial Accounting for MBAs, (Cambridge, 3rd Ed. 2013), page G-12

[15] Easton, Halsey, McAnally, Hartgraves, Morse, Financial & Managerial Accounting for MBAs, (Cambridge, 3rd Ed. 2013), page 23-13

Lesson 10: Growth Rates

Purpose: To show students how various historic growth rates can potentially affect the projection of future short-term and long-term growth rates.

Application: Use the "grow" tool found at www.businessallstars.com/calculator to find the growth rate for the company. This is the most difficult thing any analyst can do is to find a rate to use in the various models. This model analyzes growth from numerous perspectives and finds a short-term average. It also allows the user to enter a long-term growth estimate based on a combination of the change in Real GDP and the CPI.

GROWth Rates
Copyright © 2013 ACBA - All Rights Reserved
BusinessAllstars.com

Company: Dollar General (DG)   Date: 1/31/13   Calc.

#	Account	This Yr	Last Yr	2 Yrs ago	Description	Average		Recent Yr	
1.	Sales (Revenue)	16022	14807	16035	Sales Growth	0.27	%	8.21	%
2.	Net Income (NI)	953	767	628	NI Growth	23.19	%	24.25	%
3.	Dividends Pd (Div)	0	0	0	Div Growth	NaN	%	NaN	%
4.	Net Receivables (NR)	0	0	0	A/R Growth	NaN	%	NaN	%
5.	Inventory (Invn)	2397	2009	1765	Invn Growth	16.57	%	19.31	%
6.	Prop. Plant & Equip (PPE)	2089	1795	1525	PP&E Growth	17.04	%	16.38	%
7.	Total Assets (TA)	10368	9689	9546	TA Growth	4.25	%	7.01	%
8.	Common Equity (CE)	4985	4675	4054	CE Growth	10.97	%	6.63	%
9.	Operating Cashflow (CF)	1131	1050	825	CF Growth	17.49	%	7.71	%
10.	Average Price/Earnings (PE)	16.1							

Sustainable Growth	23.64 %	19.63 %	18.33 %	**AVE. S-TERM RATE**	14.17	%
Internal Growth	10.12 %	8.6 %	7.04 %	[Short-Term includes Sustainable but not Internal growth rate]		

	Real GDP %	CPI %	Nom. GDP			
Nominal GDP growth	2.37 %	2.42 %	4.79 %	**AVE. L-TERM RATE**	4.79	%

Many places on the internet and printed sources provide data about the most recent real GDP (without inflation) and the inflation rate for recent years. Here is one source that gave over ten years of recent history that was averaged for both indicators:

GDP - real growth rate (%)													
1999	2000	2001	2002	2003	2004	2005	2006	2007	2008	2009	2010	2011	Average
4.10	5.00	0.30	2.45	3.10	4.40	3.20	3.20	2.00	1.10	(2.60)	2.80	1.70	2.37

http://www.indexmundi.com/g/g.aspx?c=us&v=66

Inflation rate (consumer prices)													
1999	2000	2001	2002	2003	2004	2005	2006	2007	2008	2009	2010	2011	Average
2.20	3.40	2.80	1.60	2.30	2.50	3.20	2.50	2.90	3.80	(0.30)	1.40	3.10	2.42

http://www.indexmundi.com/g/g.aspx?v=71&c=us&l=en

GROWth Rates
Copyright © 2013 ACBA - All Rights Reserved
BusinessAllstars.com

Company: Family Dollar Stores Inc. (FDO)   Date: 8/24/12   Calc.

# Account	This Yr	Last Yr	2 Yrs ago	Description	Average		Recent Yr	
1. Sales (Revenue)	9331	8548	7867	Sales Growth	8.91	%	9.16	%
2. Net Income (NI)	422	388	358	NI Growth	8.57	%	8.76	%
3. Dividends Pd (Div)	211	182	172	Div Growth	10.87	%	15.93	%
4. Net Receivables (NR)	70	70	52	A/R Growth	17.31	%	0	%
5. Inventory (Invn)	1426	1155	1028	Invn Growth	17.91	%	23.46	%
6. Prop. Plant & Equip (PPE)	1496	1281	1112	PP&E Growth	15.99	%	16.78	%
7. Total Assets (TA)	3373	2996	2968	TA Growth	6.76	%	12.58	%
8. Common Equity (CE)	1298	1087	1422	CE Growth	-2.07	%	19.41	%
9. Operating Cashflow (CF)	369	528	591	CF Growth	-20.39	%	-30.11	%
10. Average Price/Earnings (PE)	16.2							

Sustainable Growth	23.85	%	23.38	%	15.05	%	AVE. S-TERM RATE	9.62 %
Internal Growth	8.01	%	7.38	%	6.69	%	[Short-Term includes Sustainable but not Internal growth rate]	
	Real GDP %		CPI %		Nom. GDP			
Nominal GDP growth	2.37	%	2.42	%	4.79	%	AVE. L-TERM RATE	4.79 %

Lesson 10 Exercises

10-1. Complete a GROW model for The company your instructor selects making sure the price per share and the number of shares outstanding are as of the most recent fiscal year end consistent with the financial data entered into the form.

10-2. Complete a GROW model for a public company that you have selected as the entity you intend to analyze throughout the rest of this course. Make sure the price per share and the number of shares outstanding is as of the most recent fiscal year end consistent with the financial data entered into the form.

Lesson 11: The Weighted Average Cost of Capital

Purpose: To show students how to calculate the cost of equity based on various estimation options of (1) Cost of Debt plus an equity premium; (2) the dividend discount model; and (3) the capital asset pricing model. Show how the cost of equity is combined with the cost of debt to generate the weighted average cost of capital.

Application: Use the "WACC" tool at www.businessallstars.com/calculator to find the weighted average cost of capital for a company. It employs three estimates of the cost of equity and averages the result with after-tax cost of debt for a company. An additional model "wacc" is shown where the cost of capital for a small company may be found.

WACC-Weighted Average Cost of Capital
Copyright © 2013 ACBA - All Rights Reserved
Fill in all cells even if the company has no debt

XL Name	Dollar General Corp (DG)			Date 1/31/13	Calc. WACC	8.8
Input	**Input**		**Weight**	**Output**		
D/(D+PS+CE)	15	% Tax Rate	37.25	%	Debt % (KDAT)	3.432	%
PS/(D+PS+CE)	0	% Cost of Preferred	0	%	Pref % (KPS)	0	%
Cost of Debt	5.47	% Equity Premium	5	% 33.33	% Equity % (KDEP)	10.4699999	%
Dividend Yield	0	% Growth Rate	14.17	% 33.33	% Equity % (DDM)	14.17	%
		Risk-free Rate	3.0	% 33.34	% Equity % (CAPM)	4.6	%
Beta	.20	Market Return	11	%	Equity before adj	9.746	%
Firm specific risk	0	% Size premium	0	%	Cost of Equity	9.746	%

#1 Factors affecting **Firm Specific Risk** (Up to 6%)		
Key customer dependancy	Key personel dependancy	Key supplier dependancy
Potential lawsuits	Potential regulatory changes	Potential new competition
#2 **Size Premium** up to 4% for firms of less than $2 billion in Capital		

D/(D+PS+E): Is found at the ICE model where the percentage of interest-bearing debt relative to the sum of interest-bearing debt, Preferred Stock and Common Equity.

Cost of Debt: Is found at the Bond model where the current YTM % for the Bond Rating is shown. It may also be found on various websites. One easy approach would be to us the cost of debt found at www.thatswacc.com.

Dividend Yield: The dividend yield is calculated as next year's dividend over the current stock price. This will vary from day to day and even month to month as the stock price goes up or down.

.

Beta: The beta for a company can be found at any one of several websites. They may not be consistent from one site to the other because of the basis for calculation. Generally, sixty observations of a company's performance are used, but these may be weekly, monthly or some other interval. The other

74

factor that would affect the variation in the number used is the market the company is compared against. Valueline would calculate it's beta against its own index of valueline stocks. Standard and Poor would use their market index as the basis for their calculation.

Firm Specific Risk: Is generally entered as zero unless the company has some high risk factors. These would include dependency on either: key customers; key personnel or key suppliers. It might also include the company be subject to potential lawsuits, regulatory changes or new competition. If any of these factors exist the analyst should judge the extent of the risk exposure and add a percentage in the cell from zero up to six percent.

Tax Rate: The analyst could calculate the current tax rate for a company by dividing the tax expense by the Income before taxes. The problem with this approach is that it is a point in time and may vary greatly from year to year. A better approach would be to take an average over time or use a projected number such as that found on valueline. Another easy approach would be to find the applicable tax rate on www.thatswacc.com.

Ticker Symbol: DG   [Calculate WACC]

Here is the WACC and supporting information for *Dollar General Corporation (DG)*.

You can change values in the "Your Input" sections of the tables below.

Element	From Financial Statements	Your Input
WACC:	4.38%	**4.38%**
Cost of Debt rD:	4.75%	4.75%
Corporate Tax Rate TC:	36.69%	36.69%
Total Debt D:	2,695,354,500	2,695,354,500
Total Equity E:	17,030,000,000	17,030,000,000
Total Firm Value V:	19,725,354,500	19,725,354,500
Cost of Equity rE:	4.60%	4.60%

The Cost of Equity (rE) listed above is calculated using the Capital Asset Pricing Model (CAPM) based on the values below. You can also change the assumptions in the CAPM model.
Recall that the CAPM model defines the rate of equity return as $rE = rf + B(rM - rf)$.

CAPM Component	Calculated Value:	Your Input
Beta:	0.2	0.2
Historical Market Return rm:	11.00%	11.00%
Risk Free rate rf:	3.00%	3.00%

Equity Premium: This is an estimate and based on current economic conditions could be anywhere from 4% to 6%. We have opted for a mid-range 5% estimate. This is just standard rule of thumb.

Growth Rate: The growth rate to use is typically the projected growth in dividends. Usually, financial websites will offer a rate for the next three to five years. A good place to look would be valueline.

Risk-Free Rate: This is an estimate based on current market conditions, but we have found a pretty good estimate at http://www.thatswacc.com.

.

Market Return: This is an estimate based on current market conditions, but we have found a pretty good estimate at http://www.thatswacc.com.

Size Premium: Is generally entered as zero unless the company is small relative to the chart found at the WACC model. For very small companies the rate could go as high as 4%.

Weight: The three weight factors must sum to 100% and are based on the relative significance of the three approaches to estimating the cost of equity. We usually enter 33.33%, 33.33% and 33.34% unless we feel that one or more of the approaches is terribly out of bounds, then we may enter 50%, zero, and 50% or some combination as such.

WACC-Weighted Average Cost of Capital
Copyright © 2013 ACBA - All Rights Reserved
Fill in all cells even if the company has no debt

XL	Name	Family Dollar Stores (FDO)			Date	8/24/12		Calc.	WACC	9.03	
Input		**Input**		**Weight**				**Output**			
D/(D+PS+CE)	7	% Tax Rate	36.29	%				Debt % (KDAT)	3.485		%
PS/(D+PS+CE)	0	% Cost of Preferred	0	%				Pref % (KPS)	0		%
Cost of Debt	5.47	% Equity Premium	5	%	33.33	%	Equity % (KDEP)	10.4699999		%
Dividend Yield	1.4	% Growth Rate	9.62	%	33.33	%	Equity % (DDM)	11.02		%
		Risk-free Rate	3.0	%	33.34	%	Equity % (CAPM)	6.84		%
Beta	.48	Market Return	11	%				Equity before adj	9.443		%
Firm specific risk	0	% Size premium	0	%				Cost of Equity	9.443		%

#1 Factors affecting **Firm Specific Risk** (Up to 6%)		
Key customer dependancy	Key personel dependancy	Key supplier dependancy
Potential lawsuits	Potential regulatory changes	Potential new competition
#2 **Size Premium** up to 4% for firms of less than $2 billion in Capital		

Ticker Symbol: FDO   [Calculate WACC]

Here is the WACC and supporting information for *Family Dollar Stores Inc. (FDO).*

You can change values in the "Your Input" sections of the tables below.

Element	From Financial Statements	Your Input
WACC:	6.57%	**6.57%**
Cost of Debt rD:	4.58%	4.58%
Corporate Tax Rate TC:	36.65%	36.65%
Total Debt D:	548,045,000	548,045,000
Total Equity E:	7,360,000,000	7,360,000,000
Total Firm Value V:	7,908,045,000	7,908,045,000
Cost of Equity rE:	6.84%	6.84%

The Cost of Equity (rE) listed above is calculated using the Capital Asset Pricing Model (CAPM) based on the values below. You can also change the assumptions in the CAPM model.
Recall that the CAPM model defines the rate of equity return as $rE = rf + B(rM - rf)$.

CAPM Component	Calculated Value:	Your Input
Beta:	0.48	0.48
Historical Market Return rm:	11.00%	11.00%
Risk Free rate rf:	3.00%	3.00%

KDAT formula:

After Tax Cost of Debt = Cost of Debt x (1 – Tax rate)

KDEP formula:

Cost of Debt plus Equity Premium = Cost of Debt + Equity Premium

DDM formula:

Cost of Equity = (Next Year's Dividend / Current Stock Price) + Growth

CAPM formula:

Cost of Equity = Risk-free rate + [Beta x (Market return – Risk-free rate)]

WACC formula:

WACC = (D Weight x KDAT) + (PS Weight x Preferred Cost) + (CE Weight x Cost of Equity)

Small privately held companies don't have the same issues as large publicly held corporation. So a different approach is offered to calculate the weighted average cost of their capital. On the left is the proposed average invested capital calculation for the next three to five years. This is suggested because a company is not static and the owners may depend on some level of retained earnings build-up to help finance any growth. In the center is the targeted percentage of financing from either debt (in the first group) or equity (in the second group). The total financing will equal 100% and the forced or residual percentage will go into the Other Equity category, which usually means from the owners original invested funds. The next column is for the cost of each of the sources of financing. This column is followed by the singular input for the tax rate which will be used to modify the cost of debt for an after-tax percentage.

wacc® = weighted average cost of capital (small companies)

| Name | Small Local Company | | Date | |

Net Assets (3 - 5 yr average)			Financing Capital %		Cost(m) %	Tax %	Cost %
						37.00%	
Cash	$	100	Bank Loan	20.00%	8.00%		
Acc/Rec	$	250	Credit Line	10.00%	9.00%		
Inventory	$	300	Mortgage				
Other CA	$	50	Other Debt	10.00%	7.00%		
Acc/Pay	$	150	Total Debt	40.00%	8.00%		5.04%
Net Oper Cap	$	550					
			FFF Equity	10.00%	15.00%		
Equipment	$	5,000	Angel Equity	15.00%	25.00%		
Buildings	$	1,000	VC Equity				
Land	$	-	R/E Equity	15.00%	50.00%		
Other LTAssets	$	500	Other Equity	20.00%	50.00%		
Invested Cap	$	6,500	Total Equity	60.00%	37.92%		37.92%
Total Invested Capital	$	7,050	Total Financing	100.00%		wacc	24.77%

Lesson 11 Exercises

11-1. Complete a WACC model for The company your instructor selects making sure the price per share and the number of shares outstanding are as of the most recent fiscal year end consistent with the financial data entered into the form.

11-2. Complete a WACC model for a public company that you have selected as the entity you intend to analyze throughout the rest of this course. Make sure the price per share and the number of shares outstanding is as of the most recent fiscal year end consistent with the financial data entered into the form.

Lesson 12: Traditional Valuation Methods [Part 1]

Purpose: To show students how financial ratios are comparisons of various financial data that can lead an analyst to a decision about the financial condition of a company.

Application: At www.businessallstars.com/calculator you will find the "PFC" and "CVA" tools that are traditional valuation techniques. The first is the PFC or Projected Free Cashflow Model that allows the user to project next year's Free Cash flow from the EBIT, Tax Rate NOPAT and change in Invested Capital (BV). Then growth rates are applied to the next five years cash flows with a long-term constant growth rate generating a horizon value. The value of the firm is then adjusted by subtracting debt, and adding non-operating assets. The resulting value of equity is divided by the number of shares to generate the Equity value per share.

PFC® - Projected Free Cashflow Model
Copyright © 2013 ACBA - All Rights Reserved
BusinessAllstars.com

| XL **Name** | Dollar General (DG) | | | | **Date** 1/31/13 | | Calc. |

	Current Yr	**Growth**	**Next Year**				**WACC**	
EBIT	$ 1625	14.17 %	$ 1855				8.8	%
Tax Rate			37.25 %					
NOPAT			$ 1164.01					
Invested Capital (BV)	$ 7757	4.79 %	$ 372					

	Growth		**Yr**	**Proj. FCF**	**Horizon**	**FV by Yr**	**PV by Yr**
			1	$ 792.01		$ 792.01	$ 727.95
change yr 2/yr 1	14.17	%	2	$ 904.24		$ 904.24	$ 763.88
change yr 3/yr 2	14.17	%	3	$ 1032.37		$ 1032.37	$ 801.58
change yr 4/yr 3	14.17	%	4	$ 1178.66		$ 1178.66	$ 841.15
change yr 5/yr 4	14.17	%	5	$ 1345.68	$ 38313.22	$ 39658.9	$ 26013.34
change yr 6/yr 5	14.17	%	6	$ 1536.36			----------------
L-term const. growth	4.79	%					

Value of the Firm		$ 29147.91
less Interest Bearing Debt		$ 2772
Net Equity Value		$ 26376
add Non-Operating Assets		$ 873
Gross Equity Value		$ 27249
divide by number of shares		327.07
Equity Value per share		$ 83.31

Notes:_____
_____
_____
_____

PFC® - Projected Free Cashflow Model

XL Name	Family Dollar Stores (FDO)			Date	8/24/12		Calc.

	Current Yr	Growth	Next Year			WACC	
EBIT	$ 689	9.62 %	$ 755			9.03 %	
Tax Rate			36.29 %				
NOPAT			$ 481.01				
Invested Capital (BV)	$ 1814	4.79 %	$ 87				

	Growth		Yr	Proj. FCF	Horizon	FV by Yr	PV by Yr
			1	$ 394.01		$ 394.01	$ 361.38
change yr 2/yr 1	9.62	%	2	$ 431.91		$ 431.91	$ 363.33
change yr 3/yr 2	9.62	%	3	$ 473.46		$ 473.46	$ 365.3
change yr 4/yr 3	9.62	%	4	$ 519.01		$ 519.01	$ 367.28
change yr 5/yr 4	9.62	%	5	$ 568.94	$ 14709.2	$ 15278.14000000	$ 9916.09
change yr 6/yr 5	9.62	%	6	$ 623.67		----------------	
L-term const. growth	4.79	%					

Value of the Firm	$ 11373.37
less Interest Bearing Debt	$ 516
Net Equity Value	$ 10857
add Non-Operating Assets	$ 493
Gross Equity Value	$ 11350
divide by number of shares	115.36
Equity Value per share	$ 98.39

EBIT: The Earnings-Before-Interest-and-Taxes for the Current Year comes from the Income Statement for the last fiscal year-end.

Growth (EBIT): The growth in EBIT is a projection of how much the EBIT will change between the last fiscal year-end and the

WACC: The Weighted Average Cost of Capital is the rate for all sources of external financing weighted by the optimal capital structure. This number should come from the WACC calculation taken from the www.businessallstars.com calculator and not only from www.thatswacc.com.

Tax Rate: This is the anticipated corporate income tax rate that would apply to next year. It can be taken from a calculation of the average historic, a projection at valueline or the rate used at www.thatswacc.com.

Invested Capital (BV): The ICE worksheet at www.businessallstars.com provides the number that should be used here. Use the book value and not the market value amount.

Growth (Invested Capital): Probably the most challenging rate to estimate is the growth in the book value of Invested Capital. This will have a most significant effect on the outcome of the overall calculation of the equity share price. It probably will not exceed the growth in EBIT and in many cases could be about half that rate. Nevertheless, the analyst must take care to enter a percentage that reflects the change from year to year in financing capital.

Growth (Projected Free Cash Flow): The individual year by year growth in projected free cash-flow will take the analyst out five years. Quite often this will align with the next three-to-five years change in earnings that is shown either in valueline or yahoo-finance.

Long-term constant growth: This is the rate free-cash-flow will grow indefinitely into the future. It is usually close to the nominal growth in the economy (real rate of growth plus inflation). In all cases it should be less than WACC and generally about 3% lower than WACC.

Horizon Value: The horizon value may be called the terminal or continuing value by some analysts. This number is a calculated value and represents the price for the firm at the end of the fifth year. It is the sum total of all future cash flows beyond the fifth year, discounted back to that point in time.

Value of the Firm: This field is a calculated amount and the result of adding up all the present values for the cash flows from year one through five. This represents the amount the firm could be expected to be sold for in today's dollars. It is not the acquisition of equity alone, but equity and debt.

Interest Bearing Debt: This is the current value of all interest-bearing debt and is usually found as an amount from the ICE worksheet. It includes all short and long-term debt for which there is an interest charge.

Non-Operating Assets: These are the assets that were set aside in the ICE worksheet and are not required to operate the business. It is usually excess cash and some non-operating long-term assets.

Equity Value Per Share: This is a calculated field and the result of dividing the Gross Equity Value by the number of common shares outstanding.

There are three critical formulas utilized in this worksheet:

Growth formula:

Next Year's Value = Current Year Value x (1 + growth rate)

Horizon Value formula:

Horizon Value = Next Year's free-cash-flow / (WACC – long-term growth)

Present Value formula:

Present Value = Future Value / (1 + WACC) ^ time period

CVA – Continuing Value Analysis: For some companies it is fairly difficult to project rates of change or even Free-cash flows out into the next five years. For this reason a Continuing Value Analysis approach is offered. This assumes there is a long-term constant growth rate.

CVA - Continuing Value Analysis

Copyright © 2013 ACBA - All Rights Reserved

BusinessAllstars.com

XL **Name**	Dollar General (DG)				**Date**		Calc.
	Current Yr	Growth	Next Year		**Value in today's dollars**		
EBIT	$ 1625	14.17 %	$ 1855		**Free Cash-Flow Value**	$ 23807.53	
Tax Rate		37.25 %			**Residual Income Value**	$ 23790.67	
NOPAT			$ 1164.01		less Interest Bearing Debt	$ 2772	
Invested Capital (BV)	$ 7757	Cap. Chrg.	$ 683		Net Equity Value	$ 21027	
WACC	8.8 %	Res. Inc.	$ 481.01		add Non-Operating Assets	$ 873	
L-Term growth	5.8 %				Gross Equity Value	$ 21900	
					divide by number of shares	327.07	
ROIC	15.01 %				**Equity Value per share**	$ 66.96	

The CVA above reflects a L-term growth rate that is 3% below the WACC. This is the recommended or standard differential for most companies. It results in an Equity Value per share of $66.96. Just to show how dramatic an effect a change in the growth rate that is only 2% below the WACC is the CVA below shows a Equity Value per share of $91.49.

CVA - Continuing Value Analysis

Copyright © 2013 ACBA - All Rights Reserved

BusinessAllstars.com

XL **Name**	Dollar General (DG)				**Date**		Calc.
	Current Yr	Growth	Next Year		**Value in today's dollars**		
EBIT	$ 1625	14.17 %	$ 1855		**Free Cash-Flow Value**	$ 31833.85	
Tax Rate		37.25 %			**Residual Income Value**	$ 31807.5	
NOPAT			$ 1164.01		less Interest Bearing Debt	$ 2772	
Invested Capital (BV)	$ 7757	Cap. Chrg.	$ 683		Net Equity Value	$ 29049	
WACC	8.8 %	Res. Inc.	$ 481.01		add Non-Operating Assets	$ 873	
L-Term growth	6.8 %				Gross Equity Value	$ 29922	
					divide by number of shares	327.07	
ROIC	15.01 %				**Equity Value per share**	$ 91.49	

CVA - Continuing Value Analysis

XL Name	Family Dollar Stores (FDO)			Date	8/24/12		Calc.

	Current Yr	Growth	Next Year	Value in today's dollars	
EBIT	$ 689	9.62 %	$ 755	Free Cash-Flow Value	$ 12388
Tax Rate			36.29 %	Residual Income Value	$ 12381
NOPAT			$ 481.01	less Interest Bearing Debt	$ 516
Invested Capital (BV)	$ 1814	Cap. Chrg.	$ 164	Net Equity Value	$ 11869
WACC	9.03 %	Res. Inc.	$ 317.01	add Non-Operating Assets	$ 493
L-Term growth	6.03 %			Gross Equity Value	$ 12362
				divide by number of shares	115.36
ROIC	26.52 %			Equity Value per share	$ 107.16

With a L-Term growth of 3% below WACC the Equity Value per share is $107.16. If the gap between WACC and the L-Term growth were small the value would be much higher. To test what would happen if the gap were widened to 4% the CVA below shows that result.

CVA - Continuing Value Analysis

XL Name	Family Dollar Stores (FDO)			Date	8/24/12		Calc.

	Current Yr	Growth	Next Year	Value in today's dollars	
EBIT	$ 689	9.62 %	$ 755	Free Cash-Flow Value	$ 9744.44
Tax Rate			36.29 %	Residual Income Value	$ 9739.25
NOPAT			$ 481.01	less Interest Bearing Debt	$ 516
Invested Capital (BV)	$ 1814	Cap. Chrg.	$ 164	Net Equity Value	$ 9226
WACC	9.03 %	Res. Inc.	$ 317.01	add Non-Operating Assets	$ 493
L-Term growth	5.03 %			Gross Equity Value	$ 9719
				divide by number of shares	115.36
ROIC	26.52 %			Equity Value per share	$ 84.25

Lesson 12 Exercises

12-1. Complete a PFC model for the company your instructor selects making sure the price per share and the number of shares outstanding are as of the most recent fiscal year end consistent with the financial data entered into the form.

12-2. Complete a PFC model for a public company that you have selected as the entity you intend to analyze throughout the rest of this course. Make sure the price per share and the number of shares outstanding is as of the most recent fiscal year end consistent with the financial data entered into the form.

12-3. Complete a CVA model for the company your instructor selects making sure the price per share and the number of shares outstanding are as of the most recent fiscal year end consistent with the financial data entered into the form.

12-5. Complete a CVA model for a public company that you have selected as the entity you intend to analyze throughout the rest of this course. Make sure the price per share and the number of shares outstanding is as of the most recent fiscal year end consistent with the financial data entered into the form.

Lesson 13: Traditional Valuation Methods [Part 2]

Purpose: To show students how the valuation of company stock is the result of various approached that include: (1) the dividend discount model; (2) a price to earnings model; and (3) a use of multiples model.

Application: Use the "VAL" tool at www.businessallstars.com/calculator to apply three different methods for determining the value of the company stock. The first is the Dividend Discount Model, the second the Price/Earnings Model, and the last is the Multiples Model.

VAL = Valuation Models
Copyright © 2013 ACBA - All Rights Reserved
BusinessAllstars.com

XL Name Dollar General (DG)   **Date** 1/31/13   Calc.

DIVIDEND DISCOUNT MODEL	Now	Next Year	Year +2	Year +3	Year +4	Year +5
Future Dividends per share		$0	$0	$0	$0	$0
Long-term Constant Growth	4.79 %					
Required Return on Equity	9.746 %				$0	Horizon
Present Value of Future Cash Flows		$0	$0	$0	$0	
Value of Equity Today $0						

PRICE/EARNINGS MODEL	Now	High (1)	High (2)	Low (1)	Low (2)	Average
Historic P/E Ratios past 10 years		19.5	19.3	12	13.4	16.05
Projected P/E Ratio	16.1					
Earnings Per Share	$2.87					
Value of Equity Today $46.21		Equity Value based on average historic P/E				46.06

MULTIPLES MODEL	Now	V/EBITDA	V/EBIT	V/NOPAT	P/B	P/S
Multiples		8.39	11.67	17.17	2.90	.51
Description of Base		EBITDA	EBIT	NOPAT	Book Val	Revenue
Base		$1928	$1625	$1020	$4985	$16022
Total Value (000)		$16176	$18964	$17513	$14457	$8171
Outstanding Shares (000)	327.07					
Value per share for each multiple		$49.46	$57.98	$53.55	$44.2	$24.98
Value of Equity Today $46.034						

Notes:_____

_____

_____

_____

Value Multiples by Sector

Data Used: Value Line database, of 6177 firms

Date of Analysis: Data used is as of January 2013

Variable Definitions can be obtained by clicking here

Download Detail on which companies are included in each industry

Industry Name	Number of Firms	EV/EBITDA	EV/EBIT	EV/EBIT(1-t)
Retail Automotive	19	11.03	13.74	21.12
Retail Building Supply	10	12.23	15.74	24.78
Retail Store	38	8.39	11.67	17.17
Retail/Wholesale Food	30	8.27	12.98	19.22
Securities Brokerage	27	8.79	9.85	13.62

http://pages.stern.nyu.edu/~adamodar/New_Home_Page/datafile/vebitda.html

Revenue Multiples by Sector

Data Used: Value Line database, of 6177 firms

Date of Analysis: Data used is as of January 2013

Variable Definitions can be obtained by clicking here

Download Detail on which companies are included in each industry

Industry Name	Number of Firms	Price/Sales	Net Margin	Expected Growth
Retail Automotive	19	0.66	4.24%	14.06%
Retail Building Supply	10	1.20	5.50%	17.00%
Retail Store	38	0.51	3.33%	15.35%
Retail/Wholesale Food	30	0.34	1.81%	9.66%
Securities Brokerage	27	1.57	8.05%	10.48%

http://pages.stern.nyu.edu/~adamodar/New_Home_Page/datafile/psdata.html

Price and Value to Book Ratio by Sect

Data Used: Value Line database, of 6177 firms

Date of Analysis: Data used is as of January 2013

Variable Definitions can be obtained by clicking here

Download Detail on which companies are included in each industry

Industry Name	Number of Fir	Price BV	ROE	Expected Growth in E
Retail Automotive	19	3.46	21.13%	14.06%
Retail Building Supply	10	4.32	18.11%	17.00%
Retail Store	38	2.90	18.07%	15.35%
Retail/Wholesale Food	30	3.18	16.33%	9.66%
Securities Brokerage	27	0.93	7.22%	10.48%
Automotive	12	1.26	10.02%	19.08%

http://pages.stern.nyu.edu/~adamodar/New_Home_Page/datafile/pbvdata.html

VAL = Valuation Models

XL Name	Family Dollar Stores (FDO)			Date 8/24/12		Calc.
DIVIDEND DISCOUNT MODEL	Now	Next Year	Year +2	Year +3	Year +4	Year +5
Future Dividends per share		$ .88	$ 1.01	$ 1.14000000	$ 1.27	$ 1.33
Long-term Constant Growth	4.79 %					
Required Return on Equity	9.443 %				$ 28.58	Horizon
Present Value of Future Cash Flows		$ 0.8	$ 0.84	$ 0.87	$ 20.81	
Value of Equity Today $ 23.32						

PRICE/EARNINGS MODEL	Now	High (1)	High (2)	Low (1)	Low (2)	Average
Historic P/E Ratios past 10 years		20.9	19.6	12	13.2	16.43
Projected P/E Ratio	16.2					
Earnings Per Share	$ 3.58					
Value of Equity Today $ 58		Equity Value based on average historic P/E				58.82

MULTIPLES MODEL	Now	V/EBITDA	V/EBIT	V/NOPAT	P/B	P/S
Multiples		8.39	11.67	17.17	2.90	.51
Description of Base		EBITDA	EBIT	NOPAT	Book Val	Revenue
Base		$ 900	$ 689	$ 439	$ 1298	$ 9331
Total Value (000)		$ 7551	$ 8041	$ 7538	$ 3764	$ 4759
Outstanding Shares (000)	115.36					
Value per share for each multiple		$ 65.46	$ 69.7	$ 65.34	$ 32.63	$ 41.25
Value of Equity Today $ 54.876						

TVM = Time Va

Name | Family Dollar Stores dividends paid

Standard Four Function Calculator

F		Inputs	Results
x	Rate - Interest Rate		12.91%
	Nper - Number of Periods	4	
	FV - Future Value	$ 0.78	
	PV - Present Value	$ (0.48)	
	Pmt - Annuity Payment		
	Type - Begin = 1; End = 0	0	

Dividends Paid by 8/24/12 was $.78 as per ITEM 6. SELECTED FINANCIAL DATA. Based on the TVM calculation of the annual rate change from 8/30/08 of .48 it was 12.91% per year. Applying this rate of change to $.78 it would mean a dividend in 8/25/13 of $.88 ($.78 x 1.1291). Projecting this forward three years it would be a dividend in 2016 of $1.27 ($.88 x (1.1291^3)).

ITEM 6. SELECTED FINANCIAL DATA

Summary of Selected Financial Data

| (in thousands, except per share, store, and net sales per square foot data) | | Years Ended | | | | | | | | |
		August 25, 2012		August 27, 2011		August 28, 2010		August 29, 2009		August 30, 2008
Net sales	$	9,331,005	$	8,547,835	$	7,866,971	$	7,400,606	$	6,983,628
Cost of sales		6,071,058		5,515,540		5,058,971		4,822,401		4,637,826
		3,259,947		3,032,295		2,808,000		2,578,205		2,345,802
Selling, general and administrative expenses		2,560,346		2,394,223		2,232,402		2,120,936		1,980,496
Litigation charge [1]		11,500		—		—		—		—
Operating profit		688,101		638,072		575,598		457,269		365,306
Income before income taxes		663,938		617,158		563,858		450,925		361,762
Income taxes		241,698		228,713		205,723		159,659		128,689
Net income		422,240		388,445		358,135		291,266		233,073
Diluted net income per common share	$	3.58	$	3.12	$	2.62	$	2.07	$	1.66
Dividends declared		70,302		84,342		80,394		74,013		68,537
Dividends declared per common share		0.600		0.695		0.600		0.530		0.490
Cash dividends paid		91,390		83,439		78,913		72,738		67,408
Cash dividends paid per common share		0.780		0.670		0.580		0.520		0.480
Comparable store sales growth [2]		4.7%		5.5%		4.8%		4.0%		1.2%

Lesson 13 Exercises

13-1. Complete a VAL model for the company your instructor selects making sure the price per share and the number of shares outstanding are as of the most recent fiscal year end consistent with the financial data entered into the form.

13-2. Complete a VAL model for a public company that you have selected as the entity you intend to analyze throughout the rest of this course. Make sure the price per share and the number of shares outstanding is as of the most recent fiscal year end consistent with the financial data entered into the form.

Lesson 14: Modified PEG Valuation

Purpose: To show students how a modified price to earnings to growth model can incorporate the basic elements of valuation: (1) normalized earnings; (2) risk as measured by the cost of debt; and (3) average growth as the result of short-term and long-term projections.

Application: Use the "CEM" tool at www.businessallstars.com/calculator to calculate the proposed value of stock based on the inputs. This is a model with a foundation in the PEG (Price to Earnings to Growth) relationship. It takes the PEG ratio one step further and adjusts it for risk by factoring I n the cost of debt.

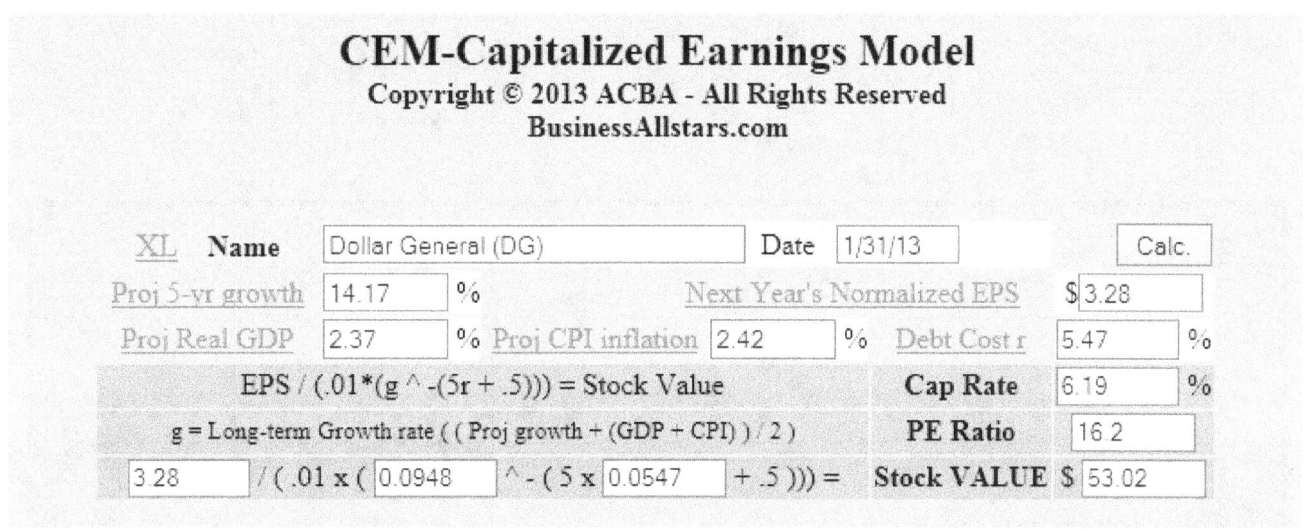

CEM-Capitalized Earnings Model
Copyright © 2013 ACBA - All Rights Reserved
BusinessAllstars.com

XL **Name** Dollar General (DG) **Date** 1/31/13 Calc.

Proj 5-yr growth 14.17 % Next Year's Normalized EPS $ 3.28

Proj Real GDP 2.37 % Proj CPI inflation 2.42 % Debt Cost r 5.47 %

EPS / (.01*(g ^ -(5r + .5))) = Stock Value **Cap Rate** 6.19 %

g = Long-term Growth rate ((Proj growth + (GDP + CPI)) / 2) **PE Ratio** 16.2

3.28 / (.01 x (0.0948 ^ - (5 x 0.0547 + .5))) = **Stock VALUE** $ 53.02

GROWth Rates
Copyright © 2013 ACBA - All Rights Reserved
BusinessAllstars.com

Company Dollar General (DG) Date 1/31/13 Calc.

# Account	This Yr	Last Yr	2 Yrs ago	Description	Average		Recent Yr	
1. Sales (Revenue)	16022	14807	16035	Sales Growth	0.27	%	8.21	%
2. Net Income (NI)	953	767	628	NI Growth	23.19	%	24.25	%
3. Dividends Pd (Div)	0	0	0	Div Growth	NaN	%	NaN	%
4. Net Receivables (NR)	0	0	0	A/R Growth	NaN	%	NaN	%
5. Inventory (Invn)	2397	2009	1765	Invn Growth	16.57	%	19.31	%
6. Prop. Plant & Equip (PPE)	2089	1795	1525	PP&E Growth	17.04	%	16.38	%
7. Total Assets (TA)	10368	9689	9546	TA Growth	4.25	%	7.01	%
8. Common Equity (CE)	4985	4675	4054	CE Growth	10.97	%	6.63	%
9. Operating Cashflow (CF)	1131	1050	825	CF Growth	17.49	%	7.71	%
10. Average Price/Earnings (PE)	16.1							

Sustainable Growth	23.64 %	19.63 %	18.33 %	**AVE. S-TERM RATE**	14.17	%
Internal Growth	10.12 %	8.6 %	7.04 %	[Short-Term includes Sustainable but not Internal growth rate]		

	Real GDP %	CPI %	Nom. GDP			
Nominal GDP growth	2.37 %	2.42 %	4.79 %	**AVE. L-TERM RATE**	4.79	%

CEM-Capitalized Earnings Model

XL	Name	Family Dollar Stores (FDO)	Date	8/24/12		Calc.

Proj 5-yr growth	9.62	%	Next Year's Normalized EPS	$ 3.96	
Proj Real GDP	2.37	% Proj CPI inflation	2.42	% Debt Cost r	5.47 %

EPS / (.01*(g ^ -(5r + .5))) = Stock Value	**Cap Rate**	7.65 %
g = Long-term Growth rate ((Proj growth + (GDP + CPI)) / 2)	**PE Ratio**	13.1

3.96	/ (.01 x (0.07205 ^ - (5 x 0.0547 + .5))) =	**Stock VALUE** $ 51.77

GROWth Rates

Company | Family Dollar Stores Inc. (FDO) | Date | 8/24/12 | Calc.

#	Account	This Yr	Last Yr	2 Yrs ago	Description	Average	Recent Yr
1.	Sales (Revenue)	9331	8548	7867	Sales Growth	8.91 %	9.16 %
2.	Net Income (NI)	422	388	358	NI Growth	8.57 %	8.76 %
3.	Dividends Pd (Div)	211	182	172	Div Growth	10.87 %	15.93 %
4.	Net Receivables (NR)	70	70	52	A/R Growth	17.31 %	0 %
5.	Inventory (Invn)	1426	1155	1028	Invn Growth	17.91 %	23.46 %
6.	Prop. Plant & Equip (PPE)	1496	1281	1112	PP&E Growth	15.99 %	16.78 %
7.	Total Assets (TA)	3373	2996	2968	TA Growth	6.76 %	12.58 %
8.	Common Equity (CE)	1298	1087	1422	CE Growth	-2.07 %	19.41 %
9.	Operating Cashflow (CF)	369	528	591	CF Growth	-20.39 %	-30.11 %
10.	Average Price/Earnings (PE)	16.2					

Sustainable Growth	23.85 %	23.38 %	15.05 %	**AVE. S-TERM RATE**	9.62 %
Internal Growth	8.01 %	7.38 %	6.69 %	[Short-Term includes Sustainable but not Internal growth rate]	

	Real GDP %	CPI %	Nom. GDP		
Nominal GDP growth	2.37 %	2.42 %	4.79 %	**AVE. L-TERM RATE**	4.79 %

Many places on the internet and printed sources provide data about the most recent real GDP (without inflation) and the inflation rate for recent years. Here is one source that gave over ten years of recent history that was averaged for both indicators:

GDP - real growth rate (%)													
1999	2000	2001	2002	2003	2004	2005	2006	2007	2008	2009	2010	2011	Average
4.10	5.00	0.30	2.45	3.10	4.40	3.20	3.20	2.00	1.10	(2.60)	2.80	1.70	2.37

http://www.indexmundi.com/g/g.aspx?c=us&v=66

Inflation rate (consumer prices)													
1999	2000	2001	2002	2003	2004	2005	2006	2007	2008	2009	2010	2011	Average
2.20	3.40	2.80	1.60	2.30	2.50	3.20	2.50	2.90	3.80	(0.30)	1.40	3.10	2.42

http://www.indexmundi.com/g/g.aspx?v=71&c=us&l=en

Capitalization Earnings Model

The Capitalization Earnings Model is a proposed simplified approach to determining the value of a company's stock. It is based on three variables: (1) The normalized Earnings of the company; (2) The long-term average growth rate for the company; and (3) the current risk adjusted cost of debt for the company.

Derivation of The Basic Formula

Peter Lynch, after retiring from a successful stint as the manager of the Magellan fund for Fidelity, wrote a book titled "One Up on Wall Street." In that book he made the statement: "The p/e ratio of any company that's fairly priced will equal its growth rate"[16] For several years Peter Lynch used the PEG ratio as a very useful metric for determining which stock to purchase. Since the publication of that book, almost all investment information services have provided the calculation of the PEG ratio as a part of their analysis.

The ratio is:

$$P/E = g$$

At first blush it seems that the ratio can't work, because the comparison is between a whole number and a decimal. Suppose the price of a share of stock is $10, the earnings $1, and the growth rate 10%. The resulting would be $10 / $1 or 10 for the P/E compared to .10 or 10 percent. Seems like it could never work, but the solution is to treat the growth rate as a whole number, so that 10% would be 10 or 20% would be 20.

After Lynch made this statement there was a lot of discussion about the advisability of using this relationship. It seemed like such a simple step to use PEG in conjunction with typical valuation methods where the most common calculations was the use of a capitalization rate (Cap Rate).

---

[16] "One Up On Wall Street," Lynch & Rothchild, Simon and Schuster, New York, 1989, page 198

Benjamin Graham said: "The most important single factor determining a stock's value is now held to be the indicated average future earning power, i.e., the estimated average earnings for a future span of years. Intrinsic value would then be found by first forecasting this earning power and then multiplying that prediction by an appropriate 'capitalization factor.'[17]

Lynch's PEG ratio can then be transformed into Graham's model by rearranging the ratio into:

(1 ÷ P/E ratio) = Cap Rate[18]

Based on the above definition of the Cap Rate and Lynch's PEG, if the price of a share were $24 and the earnings per share were $2, the growth rate should be 12%:

PEG: 24 / 2 = 12; g = 12%

Extending this relationship to a Cap Rate we divided both sides of the equal sign into one:

1 / (P / e) = e / P = 1 / g
1 / (24 / 2) = 2 / 24 or .0833

The result of these calculations is that one divided by the P/E ratio equals E/P, which also equals one over the growth rate, which in turn is equal to the Cap Rate. Shannon Pratt talked about these relationships, but used cash flow in place of earnings: "The expected growth rate in perpetuity for cash flow translates point for point into the capitalization rate for the variable. The guideline company indicated price/cash flow multiple is 8, results in a capitalization rate for cash flow of 12.5 percent [1 / 8 = 12.5%]."[19]

His discussion points to the close relationship between Cap Rates and growth. The unique perspective that Lynch offers, where P/E equals growth, can have a dramatic impact on the Cap Rate. Table #1 shows how the growth rate is translated into the Cap Rate.

Table #1

Growth Rate (g)	1/g (Cap Rate)
.05	.200
.10	.100
.15	.067
.20	.050
.25	.040
.30	.033

Plotting this relationship generates the graph depicted below:

Graph #1

[17] Benjamin Graham, David L. Dodd, & Sidney Cottle, "Security Analysis: Principles and Techniques," McGraw-Hill, New York, 1962, pg 28

[18] "http://www.bus.ucf.edu/weaver/BV%20&%20Litigation%20Support%20 Articles/articles/businessvaluationtechniques.htm"

[19] "Valuing a Business: The Analysis and Appraisal of Closely held Companies," Pratt, Reilly, & Schweihs, 3rd Edition, Irwin, Chicago, 1996, page 226

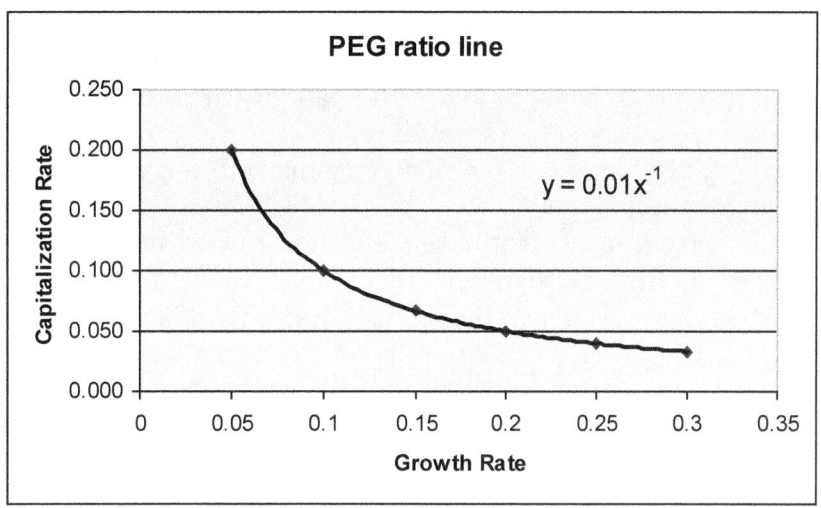

This relationship seemed to have worked well for Lynch in the 1980s. The formula as defined by the line in the graph would be interpreted as:

$$y = .01x^{-1}$$

where

y = the Cap Rate
x = growth rate

Substituting for y and x the formula is restated as:

Cap Rate = $.01g^{-1}$

Applying this formula we can see how it affects the Price of a company's stock. Suppose a company has Earnings per share of $2.00 and an estimated growth rate of 5%. The price of the company should be:

Price = ESP / $.01g^{-1}$

Where the calculation of the Cap Rate is:

$.20 = .01 \times .05^{-1} = .01g^{-1}$

And the price of the stock would be:

$10.00 = $2.00 / .20

This is a relationship that is totally based on the PEG ratio. But what happens when interest rates move and are much lower. Is the fundamental PEG ratio still a sound measure of value?
Paul Tracy has suggested: "Of course, bullish market observers argue that times have changed. Specifically, they believe that some of these older valuation models are less relevant today because

interest rates are so low. According to an economic model of stock valuations known as the Fed Model, lower interest rates can help support higher valuation levels in the market."[20]

Damodaran supports this challenge to the PEG ratio when he stated that there are problems with comparing PE ratios to expected growth. He said[21]
- In its simple form, there is no basis for believing that a firm is undervalued just because it has a PE ratio less than expected growth.
- This relationship may be consistent with a fairly valued or even an overvalued firm, if interest rates are high, or if a firm is high risk.
- As interest rate decrease (increase), fewer (more) stocks will emerge as undervalued using this approach.

A simple test of historical data seems to support the theory that as interest rates fall the PEG ratio may undervalue a stock. We gathered data from Damodaran's web site for historical expected growth and Cap Rates. A plot of four years shows that the PEG line might well be lower as interest rates fall.

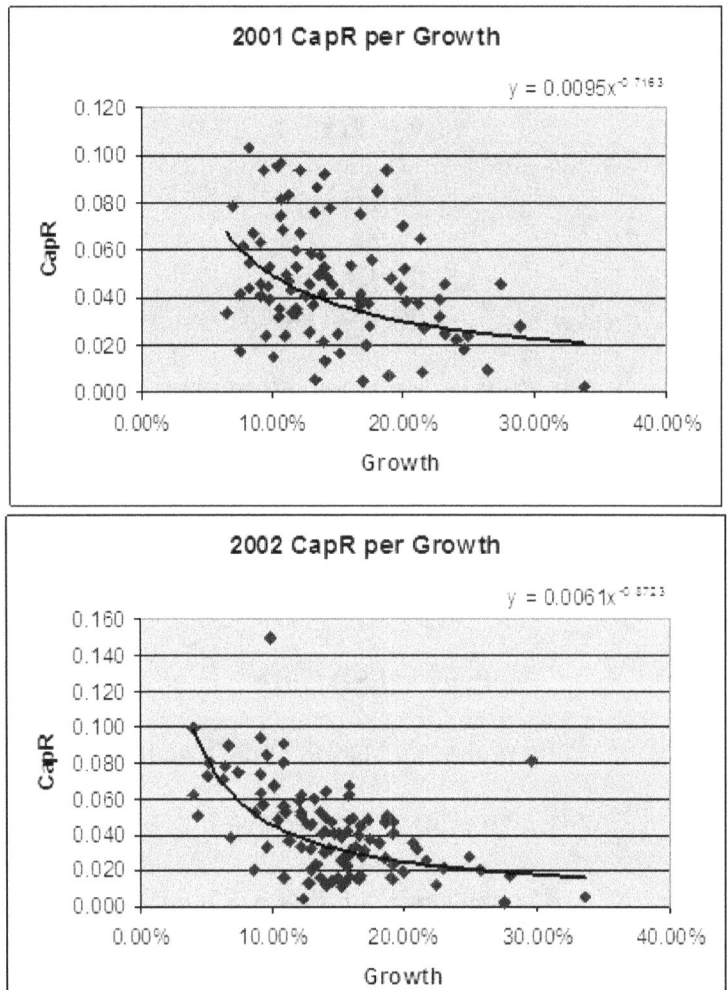

[20] http://www.zacks.com/experts/featured/view_article.php?art_id=1587&newsletter_id=148
[21] http://pages.stern.nyu.edu/~adamodar/New_Home_Page/lectures/peg.htm

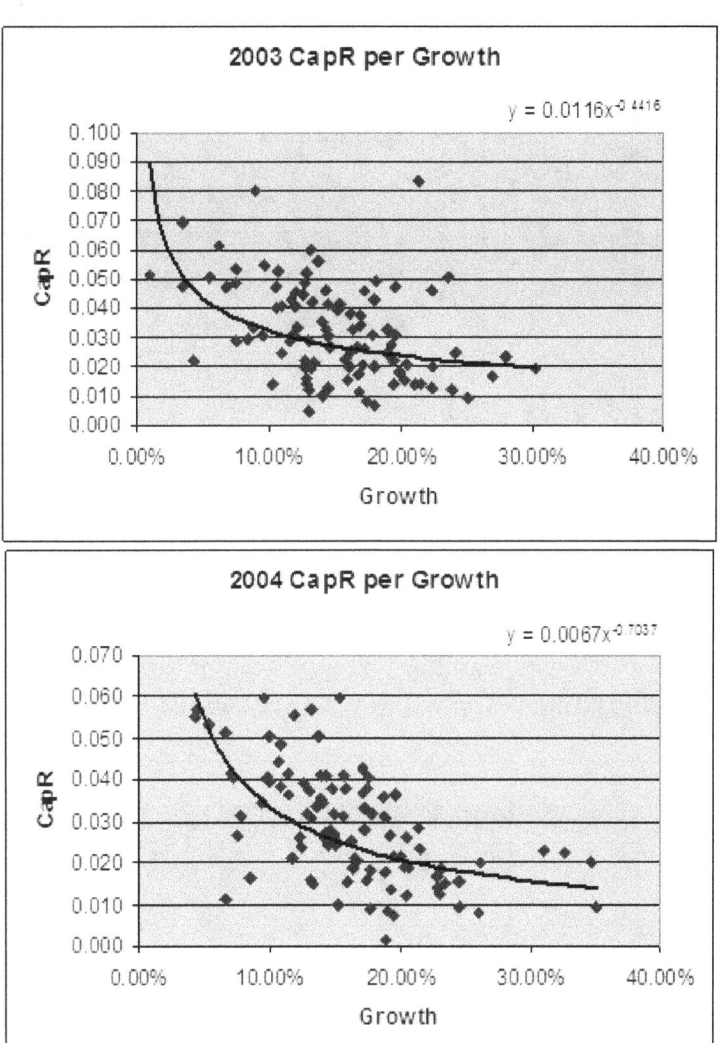

These are just a sample of the universe of possibilities. Realizing "the valuation of a privately owned company is both science and art,"[22] and through trial and error, we have taken the liberty to modify the PEG line for what we feel is a rational and justifiable modification to allow for the change in interest rates. The resulting formula, or Bunker Curve:

$$\textbf{Cap Rate} = \textbf{.01 x } g^{-(5 \text{ x r} + .5)}$$

Table #2 and Graph #6

---

[22] http://www.vrbusinessbrokers.com/pages/mergers/valuation_services.jsp
95

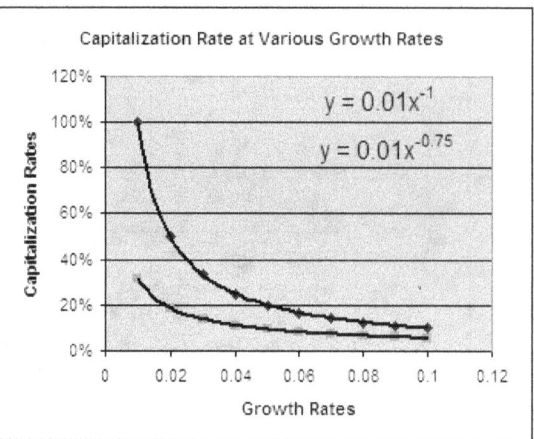

	Int Rate 10%	Int Rate 5%
Growth	CapR	CapR
0.01	100%	31.62%
0.02	50%	18.80%
0.03	33%	13.87%
0.04	25%	11.18%
0.05	20%	9.46%
0.06	17%	8.25%
0.07	14%	7.35%
0.08	13%	6.65%
0.09	11%	6.09%
0.1	10%	5.62%

The above table and graph show that by applying the Bunker Curve and formula, when the interest rates drop the whole curve drops to a lower level. The result is that for each growth rate the related Capitalization Rate is lower. This in turn will increase the price of stock for any given earnings level.

We feel this is a significant change and is a simple straight forward approach that incorporates both estimated growth and interest rates. Applied to what we call the Capitalized Earnings Modelor CRM the result is:

$$\text{Value} = \text{ESP} / .01 \times g^{-(5 \times r + .5)}$$

Using the Model

Several challenges arise in the use of such a model. First is the issue of using Earnings or Earnings per share to determine value. Forbes magazine had a recent article that stated: "If push come to shove, and the chairman wants a nickel more per share, any good controller knows where to find it."[23]

Basing the price of a stock of a single earnings number for the next period is a challenge. Mulford and Comisky wrote: "It is important, for both the producers and the users of financial statements, to know whether earnings management techniques fall within or outside the boundaries of GAAP [Generally Accepted Accounting Principles]."[24]

Add to this the comments by Schilit that "Companies in hot water are often quite sophisticated at using 'creative accounting' techniques to disguise damaging information and provide a distorted picture of their financial health."[25] There should be significant skepticism over the number to be used.

There is no easy answer to finding if the company has employed creating accounting techniques to manipulate the bottom line. It has been our experience that almost all companies do it. Most recently (post Sarbanes-Oxley), we sat in the board meeting of a small company where the auditors openly acknowledged that they approved the use of "Cookie Jar" techniques to allow for the smoothing of earnings.

Normalized Earnings

---

[23] Dana Wechster Linden, "Lies of the bottom line," Forbes Magazine, November 12, 1990, pg 112
[24] Charles W. Mulford and Eugene E. Comiskey, "The Financial Numbers Game: Detecting Creative Accounting Practices," John Wiley & Sons, Inc., New York, 2002, pg 62
[25] Howard M. Schilit, "Financial Shenanigans: How to Detect Accounting Gimmicks & Fraud in Financial Reports," McGraw-Hill, Inc., New York, 1993, front fly-leaf

Damodaran addressed the issue of averaging when he wrote: "One solution [for negative cyclical earnings] is to use an average-earnings-per-share over a time period long enough to span an economic cycle as the earnings in the base year. This average-earnings-per-share is considered 'normalized' because it takes into account the cyclicality."[26]

The purpose in normalizing earnings is that because we are using a single earnings estimate, for the next period, to represent all out years, we have to be sure it is representative of the companies normal on-going earnings potential. Several authors have proposed making a few minor adjustments to find the best number.

The Portable MBA states: "After the valuator identifies the adjustments [for unusual or non-recurring items and expenses not reflecting market values] the reported earnings of the company are modified to reflect the economic earnings of the business on an ongoing basis."[27]

Any officer's compensation that includes a hidden dividend should be adjusted as well as any adjustments for non-arm length transactions to bring them to market value. The earnings figure that is used as the base-year number should reflect the normal earning potential of the company that can be carried forward into subsequent years.

Normalizing earnings is a critical step for valuation purposes. Unfortunately, when a stock is priced in the market place investors don't usually normalize the numbers. Since we are trying to determine how the market would price the stock, we usually just use analyst's estimates.

Growth Rates

Damodaran's Basic Premise is that the infinite growth rate cannot exceed the growth rate for the overall economy (GNP) by more than a small amount (1-2%). He estimates the upper limit for the United States as the long term inflation rate of 5% + real GNP growth of 3% = 8%. The lower end is estimated to be the long term inflation rate of 3% + real GNP growth of 2% = 5%.[28]

Benjamin Graham takes a little different position when he stated in his classic work that "we set forth our opinion that a permanent growth rate exists in investment-quality common stock in general, and we further stated that this growth might be estimated conservatively at 3½ percent per annum."[29]

Robert S. Harris provided additional information about extended growth patterns when he wrote: "Initial years of growth were based on Value Line's five-year earnings growth forecasts with subsequent growth approaching a long-run real national growth rate of 4%."[30]

Damodaran is much more contemporary than either Graham who wrote in the 1940s to 1960s or Harris who wrote in 1986. We conclude that the long-term rate would be between 3½% and 8% depending on conditions and prospects.

Our approach has been to take current economic forecasts for two years out. A recent forecast estimated annual Real GDP to be 3.0% with a CPI Inflation estimate of 3.5%. Combined, the long-term growth rate would be 6.5%.

Balancing short-term and long-term

---

[26] Aswath Damodaran, "Investment Valuation: Tools and techniques for determining the value of any asset," John Wiley & Sons, New York, 1996, pg 269

[27] Edited by John Leslie Livingston and Theodore Grossman, "The Portable MBA: in Finance and Accounting," Third Edition, John Wiley & Sons, Inc., New York, 2002, pg 608

[28] http://pages.stern.nyu.edu/~adamodar/New_Home_Page/lectures/ddm.html

[29] Benjamin Graham, David L. Dodd, and Sidney Cottle, "Security Analysis: Principles and Techniques," Fourth Edition, McGraw-Hill book company, New York, 1962, pg 470

[30] Robert S. Harris, "Using Analysts' Growth Forecasts to Estimate shareholder Required Rate of Return." Financial Management; Spring 1986, pg 58-67

McKinsey uses a model in their text on Valuation where they forecast an explicit period of ten years and then add a continuing value for years beyond that period. About thirty percent of the total value of the company is driven by the explicit period, while about seventy percent is driven by the continuing value.

Comparing this to Damodaran's Valuation text where he describes a two-stage model and we find that the first or early stage accounts for about 20% of the total value. The constant growth stage beyond that point accounts for about 80%.

Several authors have continually suggested that the impact of the early stage is totally dependent on how long it lasts. Both Valueline and Yahoo Financial make an estimate of the next five years growth. Many other services do the same. Using an estimate for the near term and another for the longer-term "Constant" stage, the only question that would remain is how to weight the two.

David Durand discussed the balance between the short and long terms when he said: "Growth, when defined as expansion through the exploitation of supernormal opportunities, is a temporary imperfection; it must pass away with the arrival of the long-run equilibrium, though that may be a long time coming. Growth stocks, too, are a temporary phenomenon, for they are characterized by supernormal returns with prices above book value; many of them, moreover, are relatively short-lived in terms of the long future before the long-run equilibrium sets in. The growth-stock investor's challenge then is to strike the right balance between optimism and skepticism in forecasting for each stock how long the party can last."[31]

It is extremely difficult to know how long a strong short-term growth pattern will last without expert analysis. We have determined to simply us a balanced approach where we give half the weight to the short term and half to the long-term. Using this approach we would extract a short term projection for a sample company of 10.5%. Matching this with a long-term average of GDP and inflation of 6% we would get:

$$(50\% \times 10.5\%) + (50\% \times 6.0\%) = 8.25\%$$

Interest Rates

In Homer and Sylla's wonderful examination of interest rates through history they stated: "Credit long antedated industry, banking, and even coinage; it probably antedated primitive forms of money. Loans at interest may be said to have begun when the Neolithic farmer made a loan of seed to a cousin and expected more back at harvest-time. Be this as it may, we know that the recorded legal history of several great civilizations started with elaborate regulations of credit."[32]

They continued by saying: "A comprehensive view of the history of interest rates will unsettle most preconceived ideas of what is a high rate or a low rate or an average rate. Each generation tends to consider as normal the range of interest rates with which it grew up; rates much higher suggest a crisis or seem extortionate, while rates much lower seem artificial or inadequate. Almost every generation is eventually shocked by the behavior of interest rates because, in fact, market rates of interest in modern times rarely have been stable for long. Usually they are rising or falling to unexpected extremes. Students of the history of interest rates will not be surprised by volatility. Their backward-looking knowledge will not tell them where interest rates will be in the future, but it will permit them to distinguish a truly unusual level of rates from a mere change."[33]

---

[31] David Durand, "Afterthoughts on a Controversy with MM, Plus New Thoughts on Growth and the Cost of Capital," Financial Management; Summer 1989, pg 12-18

[32] Sidney Homer and Richard Sylla, "A History of Interest Rates," Third Edition, Revised, Rutgers University Press, New Brunswick, New Jersey, 1996, pg 3

We have struggled to determine the proper interest rate to use in the Capitalized Earnings Model (CEM). Because we utilize an average of short-term and long-term growth rates to arrive at the single growth number to use, we should probably be consistent and use the same approach for interest rate. We abandoned this approach for one simple reason. The valuation for most companies is based on their current credit status and the rate at which they can reasonably finance their debt. For this reason we utilize their current debt rating and its related interest rate.

Testing the Model

Many tests have been conducted using the model to determine the value of a company, but a few were of significance. The first was conducted on May 18th, 2005. We listed all of the stocks in the S&P 500 and gathered their estimated earnings per share for next year and their projected 5-year growth rate from Yahoo Financial. We then assumed an average 5% interest rate across the board. The default average interest rate was used because of the difficulty in gathering the average bond rating for each company.

We then assumed a long-term growth rate for the economy in total of 6%. A simple average of the long-term growth in the economy and the company specific 5-year projected growth gave us the growth rate that was used in the Capitalized Earnings Model for each company.

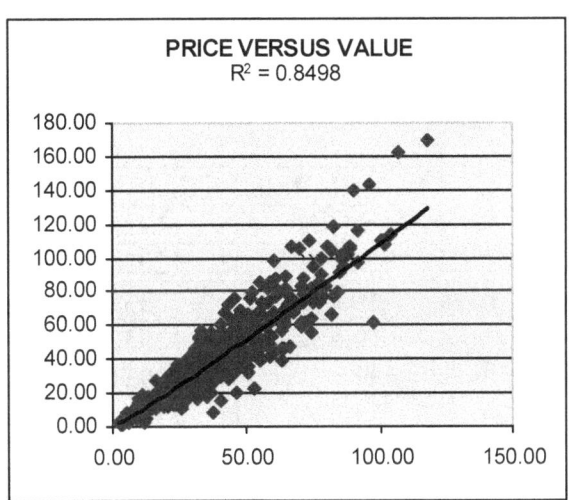

After applying the average growth rate, the projected EPS, and an average 5% interest rate to the Capitalized Earnings Model we generated a proposed value for each company's stock. The first pass in calculating the r-square for the price and value resulted in .8248. The greatest discrepancies appeared to be in two areas: (1) financial institutions, and (2) real estate/home building related companies. We removed those two groups from the test and plotted the current price of the stock against the calculated value again. The resulting r-squared was .8498. We felt the test was relatively successful.

S&P 500 index

[33] Sidney Homer and Richard Sylla, "A History of Interest Rates," Third Edition, Revised, Rutgers University Press, New Brunswick, New Jersey, 1996, pg 4

We asked ourselves if the model could be used to generate a value for an index. To test this we decided to look at the S&P 500 index. From a recent BusinessWeek we went to the page for "Figures of the Week[34]." The S&P 500 stood at 1270.3 with a P/E Ratio (Next 12 mos.) of 14.7. These two numbers gave us a projection of what we called the Earnings per Index or EPI of $86.41. The short-term 5-year growth rate was projected to be 10.5%, based on Yahoo Financial[35]. The Conference Board's Web site[36] gave us a projected Real GDP of 2.5 and CPI Inflation projection of 3.2, which added to a long-term economic growth projection of 5.7%. If an interest rate of 5.3% was used the Capitalized Earnings Model resulted in a value of the S&P 500 index of 1263.4. We felt good about the result but also realized that a few minor changes to some of the estimates could have a fairly significant impact on the value.

Given that we were in a period where the Fed was raising interest rates, and if the rate we used went up the results could be dramatic:

Interest Rate	CRM Value
5.3%	1263.4
5.5%	1238.1
5.7%	1201.5
5.9%	1171.7
6.1%	1142.6

On the other hand if the interest rate were left at 5.3% and the growth rate projection were changed either up or down the impact would be:

Growth Rate	CRM Value
9.0%	1172.9
9.5%	1203.3
10.0%	1233.5
10.5%	**1263.4**
11.0%	1293.2
11.5%	1322.7
12.0%	1352.0

We felt the model did a very nice job of showing the impact of changes in the various components on the index value. This led us to wonder how the model would fare when applied to historical data.

Historical Analysis

First we found the S&P500 year-end price from 1960 to 2000. Then we started gathering data for the Capitalization Rate Model. We found the change in the CPI and Real GDP for the same period. We used this as an estimate of the overall growth in the economy. Next we found the P/E ratio for each year and assumed this was an estimate of short-term growth. Then the overall growth in the economy and short-term growth were averaged to approximate growth for the model.

---

[34] BusinessWeek, May 29th, 2006, page 102
[35] http://finance.yahoo.com/q/ae?s=HD
[36] http://www.conference-board.org/economics/stalk.cfm

We then found the Earnings per the Index for each year and projected what the next year would be based on the growth rate. This gave us an estimate of the next year's earnings. We used the AAA bond rate for each year to give us an approximation of the interest rate to use. With our components in place we applied the model to generate a value for the S&P 500 for each year from 1960 to 2000.

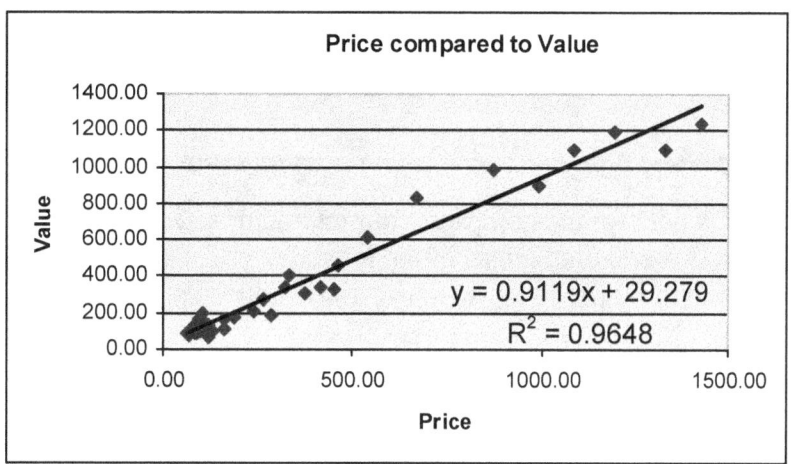

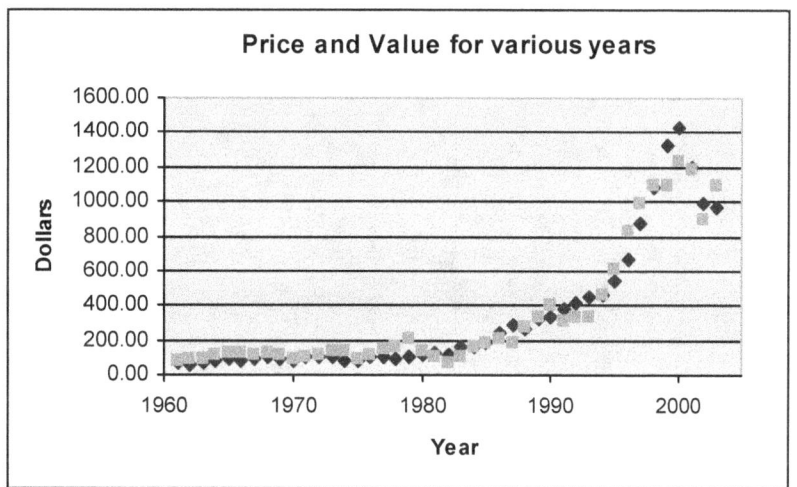

The accompanying graphs show the results of our comparison. While there was quite a difference in some years and for some periods the value ran consistently higher or lower than the year end price, the overall analysis seemed reasonable. The resulting r-squared was .9648, which seemed to indicate the model had some validity.

Conclusion

The Capitalized Earnings Model is in its early stages of development and review, but seems to suggest there is a potential for the use in valuation. It employs significantly fewer assumptions than most valuations models and appears to be easier to apply. It places heavy reliance on the three variables of Normalized Earnings per Share, the long-term average growth rate, and the risk adjusted interest rate for the company, but these all seem to be the most commonly expressed metrics in the financial media. Hopefully, continue review and development will produce a tool that will be of value.

Lesson 14 Exercises

14-1. Complete a CEM model for the company your instructor selects making sure the price per share and the number of shares outstanding are as of the most recent fiscal year end consistent with the financial data entered into the form.

14-2. Complete a CEM model for a public company that you have selected as the entity you intend to analyze throughout the rest of this course. Make sure the price per share and the number of shares outstanding is as of the most recent fiscal year end consistent with the financial data entered into the form.

Lesson 15: Break-Even Revenue

Purpose: To show students how break-even can be used to evaluate a company performance when incorporating a capital charge and residual income. Calculate the operating break-even revenue and the global break-even revenue.

Application: Use the "BER" tool at www.businessallstars.com/calculator to find the global break-even revenue and the operating break-even revenue. By use of a regression of the expenses against the revenue per quarter variable cost % and a fixed cost amount can be found. If the regression fails to generate a satisfactory result a default position is calculated as all costs of revenue will be treated as variable costs and all other operating costs as fixed cost. The User should chose which is more relevant, the regression or the "cost of revenue" method.

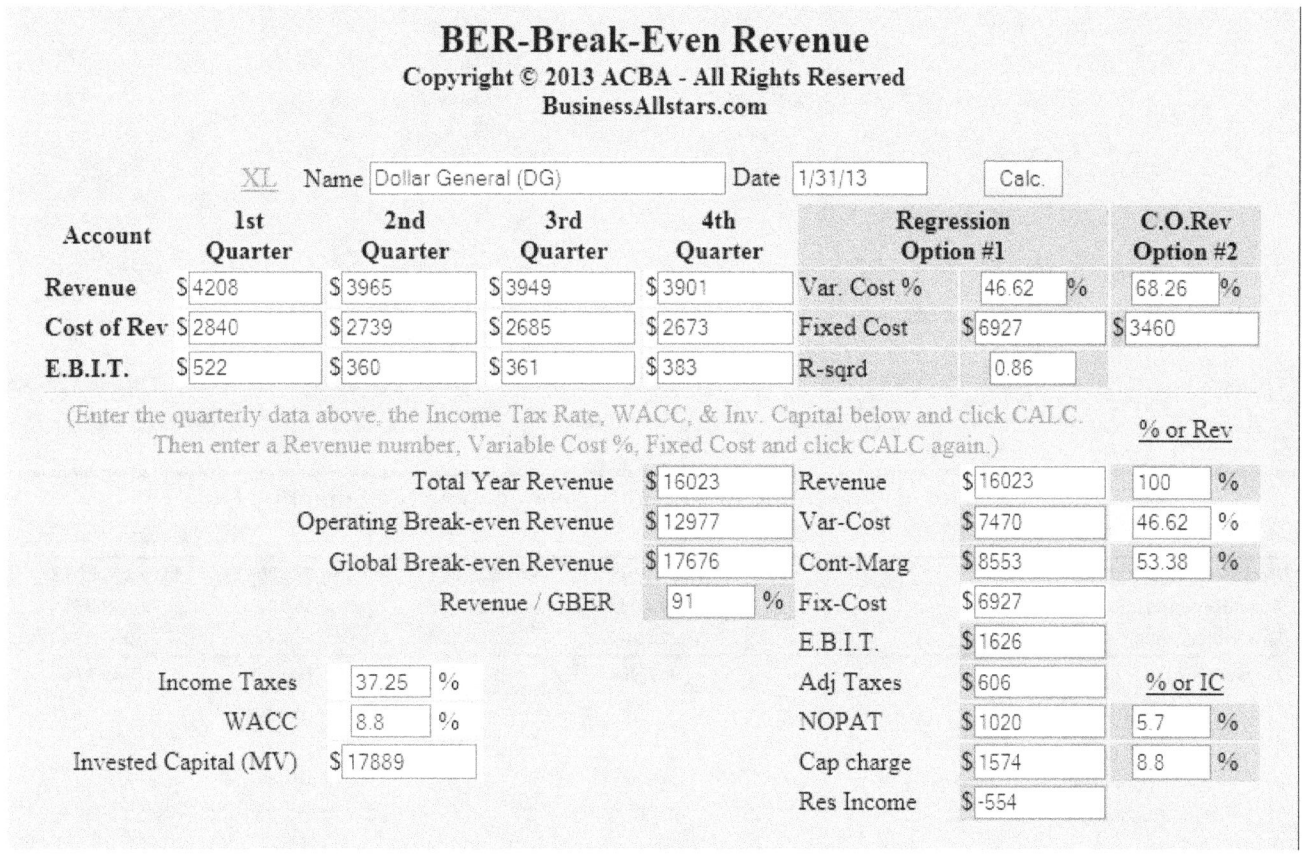

Quarterly Data is taken from the 10-K at Free Edgar

(In thousands)	First Quarter	Second Quarter	Third Quarter	Fourth Quarter
2012:				
Net sales	$ 3,901,205	$ 3,948,655	$ 3,964,647	$ 4,207,621
Gross profit	1,228,256	1,263,223	1,226,123	1,367,799
Operating profit	384,324	387,214	361,389	522,349
Net income	213,415	214,140	207,685	317,422
Basic earnings per share	0.64	0.64	0.62	0.97
Diluted earnings per share	0.63	0.64	0.62	0.97

http://yahoo.brand.edgar-online.com/displayfilinginfo.aspx?FilingID=9181907-1014-521083&type=sect&dcn=0001047469-13-003283

BER-Break-Even Revenue

XL Name Family Dollar Stores (FDO) Date 8/24/12 [Calc.]

Account	1st Quarter	2nd Quarter	3rd Quarter	4th Quarter	Regression Option #1		C.O.Rev Option #2	
Revenue	$ 2894	$ 2422	$ 2364	$ 2360	Var. Cost %	87.3 %	65.75 %
Cost of Rev	$ 1927	$ 1595	$ 1564	$ 1515	Fixed Cost	$ 584	$ 2748	
E.B.I.T.	$ 225	$ 133	$ 133	$ 200	R-sqrd	0.98		

(Enter the quarterly data above, the Income Tax Rate, WACC, & Inv. Capital below and click CALC. Then enter a Revenue number, Variable Cost %, Fixed Cost and click CALC again.)

% or Rev

				% or Rev
Total Year Revenue	$ 10040	Revenue	$ 10040	100 %
Operating Break-even Revenue	$ 4598	Var-Cost	$ 8765	87.3 %
Global Break-even Revenue	$ 13200	Cont-Marg	$ 1275	12.7 %
Revenue / GBER	76 %	Fix-Cost	$ 584	
		E.B.I.T.	$ 691	
Income Taxes	36.29 %	Adj Taxes	$ 251	% or IC
WACC	9.03 %	NOPAT	$ 440	5.71 %
Invested Capital (MV)	$ 7709	Cap charge	$ 696	9.03 %
		Res Income	$ -256	

Quarterly Data can also be found at Yahoo finance Income Statement by Quarter

View: Annual Data | **Quarterly Data**   All numbers in thousands

Period Ending	Mar 1, 2013	Nov 23, 2012	Aug 24, 2012	May 25, 2012
Total Revenue	**2,893,997**	**2,421,688**	**2,364,125**	**2,359,957**
Cost of Revenue	1,926,947	1,594,894	1,564,422	1,514,684
Gross Profit	**967,050**	**826,794**	**799,703**	**845,273**
Operating Expenses				
Research Development	-	-	-	-
Selling General and Administrative	750,073	699,825	655,546	635,165
Non Recurring	-	-	11,500	-
Others	-	-	-	-
Total Operating Expenses	-	-	-	-
Operating Income or Loss	**216,977**	**126,969**	**132,657**	**210,108**
Income from Continuing Operations				
Total Other Income/Expenses Net	7,535	6,437	211	(10,428)
Earnings Before Interest And Taxes	224,512	133,406	132,868	199,680

http://finance.yahoo.com/q/is?s=FDO

104

Lesson 15 Exercises

15-1. Complete a BER model for The company your instructor selects making sure the price per share and the number of shares outstanding are as of the most recent fiscal year end consistent with the financial data entered into the form.

15-2. Complete a BER model for a public company that you have selected as the entity you intend to analyze throughout the rest of this course. Make sure the price per share and the number of shares outstanding is as of the most recent fiscal year end consistent with the financial data entered into the form.

Lesson 16: Mergers and Acquisitions

Purpose: To show students how a merger and acquisition template can lead to the combination of an acquiring and target companies. Demonstrate the summary of other analytical tools to generate the needed data for the analysis.

Application: At the http://www.businessallstars.com/software/summary.html web location is found a Summary of Analysis where data from the various models is pulled together to form an overall picture of the company. This is an excellent reference to check that the data used in each model is consistent.

Students will compare the data for two companies that may be merger or acquisition candidates. By looking at the data they will make a decision as to which company is stronger and may be the potential acquiring company or which may end up as the target company. This will lead to the M&A model that is found in at www.businessallstars.com/calculator. A student team will make the decision regarding the merger or acquisition and complete the M&A model proposing a source of financing, broken out into a percentage from Excess Cash Equivalents, A/P – (A/R + Inv) or Int-Bearing Liabilities. A decision will then be made regarding if the Target Int-Bearing Liabilities will be eliminated or carried forward. If they will be eliminated the small box in the upper right hand corner will need to have a "yes" enter in it. The next decisions will be what the Offering Price for the target company's stock will be and if there will be any efficiency from the combined operation that will result in an increase in the EBIT that will be generated.

M&A-Mergers & Acquisitions
Copyright © 2013 ACBA - All Rights Reserved
BusinessAllstars.com

XL Companys	DG		FDO		If eliminating Target Int-Bear. Liab enter yes?			
	Target	**%**	**Acquiring**	**%**	**Fin Source**	**Combined Co**		**%**
Excess Cash Equivalents	$ -179		$ 38		0	%	$ -141	
A/P - (A/R + Inv)	$ -659		$ -438		0	%	$ -1097	
Goodwill							$ 14639	
Invested Capital	$ 7757	**Cap Str**	$ 1814	**Cap Str**			$ 24210	**Cap Str**
Int-Bearing Liabilities	$ 2772	15.5 %	$ 516	6.69 %	0	%	$ 3288	12.28 %
Book Value of Equity	$ 4985		$ 1298		100	%	$ 20922	
Number of Shares O/S	327.07		115.36		**Offr Price**		$ 430	
Stock Price	$ 46.22		$ 62.35		$ 60		$ 54.64	
Market Value of Equity	$ 15117	84.5 %	$ 7193	93.31 %			$ 23495	87.72 %
Total to be funded	$ 19624.2	**Other %**		**Other %**	**Incr. EBIT**			**Average %**
E.B.I.T.	$ 1855		$ 755		5	%	$ 2741	
Interest Expense	$ 128	4.62 %	$ 25	4.84 %			$ 153	4.65 %
Taxes	$ 691	40.01 %	$ 274	37.53 %			$ 1017	39.28 %
Net Income	$ 1036		$ 456				$ 1571	
Earnings Per Share	$ 3.17		$ 3.95				$ 3.65	
Price / Earnings	14.58		15.78				14.97	Calc.

Lesson 16 Exercises

16-1. Complete a Summary and a M&A model for The company your instructor selects making sure the price per share and the number of shares outstanding are as of the most recent fiscal year end consistent with the financial data entered into the form.

16-2. Complete a Summary and a M&A model for a public company that you have selected as the entity you intend to analyze throughout the rest of this course. Make sure the price per share and the number of shares outstanding is as of the most recent fiscal year end consistent with the financial data entered into the form.

Lesson 17: Cash, Capital Budgeting and BIND

Purpose: Demonstrate the implementation of a monthly cash projection that will lead to data to be used in a capital budgeting template. The template will result in the calculation of: (1) BCR or the benefit to cost ratio [profitability index]; (2) IRR or the internal rate of return; (3) NPV or the net present value; and (4) DPB or the discounted payback period.

Application: At the web site www.businessallstars.com/calculator the models for "Cash, CBUD, and BIND" provide tools to perform capital budgeting analysis. The Cash model required the user to think through the various detail revenues and expenses for a year. The CBUD model then allows the user to enter fundamental assumptions that will result in a five year cash flow analysis with decision metrics. BIND is a simple calculation of metrics from projected free cash flows.

CASH Budget 12-Month Model - Year #1

Investment: $ 5,000.00   Life: 5   Depr: 20.0%   R/Repl %: 5.0%   Days: 20   Tax %: 25.0%

	Rev	COS	Sal/Wages	Benefits	Prof Fees	Travel	Rent	Utilities	Supplies	R&D	Marketing	Other
$/unit	6.00	1.00	2.00	0.30	0.00	0.00	0.00	0.00	0.20	0.20	0.60	0.60
$/mon	0	0	80	24	20	20	40	8	4	10	8	20

Months	1	2	3	4	5	6	7	8	9	10	11	12
Units sold	80	160	250	250	400	500	500	500	400	200	200	160
Revenue	480	960	1,500	1,500	2,400	3,000	3,000	3,000	2,400	1,200	1,200	960
Cost of Sales	80	160	250	250	400	500	500	500	400	200	200	160
Gross Profit	400	800	1,250	1,250	2,000	2,500	2,500	2,500	2,000	1,000	1,000	800
Salaries/Wages	240	400	580	580	880	1,080	1,080	1,080	880	480	480	400
Benefits	48	72	99	99	144	174	174	174	144	84	84	72
Fees	20	20	20	20	20	20	20	20	20	20	20	20
Travel	20	20	20	20	20	20	20	20	20	20	20	20
Rent	40	40	40	40	40	40	40	40	40	40	40	40
Utilities	8	8	8	8	8	8	8	8	8	8	8	8
Supplies	20	36	54	54	84	104	104	104	84	44	44	36
Research/Devel.	26	42	60	60	90	110	110	110	90	50	50	42
Marketing	56	104	158	158	248	308	308	308	248	128	128	104
Other Expense	68	116	170	170	260	320	320	320	260	140	140	116
EBITDA	(146)	(58)	41	41	206	316	316	316	206	(14)	(14)	(58)
Work Cap adj:	316	316	355	-	592	395	-	-	(395)	(789)	-	(158)
Renew/Repl adj:			63			63			63			63
Depr Tax Shield:			(63)			(63)			(63)			(63)
Taxes:			41			(141)			(210)			22
Net Cash Flow	(462)	(374)	(292)	41	(386)	125	316	316	873	775	(14)	141
Cum Cash Flow	(462)	(835)	(1,128)	(1,087)	(1,472)	(1,348)	(1,032)	(716)	157	932	918	1,059

Total Units:	3,600	Var Cost per Unit:	4.90	NOIC changes:	881.23
Revenue per Unit:	6.00	Fixed Cost:	2,808	NOIC % of Rev:	4.1%

Notes:_____

_____

_____

_____

CBUD - Capital Budgeting Model

Assumptions

Initial depreciable investment:	5,000.00	Initial Non-Depr. Investment:			0
1st year units:	3600	Growth:	5.0%	5.0%	5.0%	5.0%
Sales price per unit:	6.00	Inflation Assumption:			3.0%
Variable cost per unit;	4.90	First Year Fixed Cost:			2808
Deprec (3,5,7,10,15 or 20):	5	20.0%	32.0%	19.2%	11.5%	11.5%
Tax Rate:	25.0%	Salvage Value:			1000
NOIC chng. % of Revenue:	4.1%	Weighted Avg Cost of Capital:			10.0%

BCR	1.11	IRR	13.6%	NPV	671	DPB	4.72

	0	1	2	3	4	5
Initial Investment	-5000					
Units Sold		3600	3780	3969	4167	4376
Revenue		21600	23360	25264	27323	29550
Variable Costs		-17640	-19078	-20632	-22314	-24133
Fixed Costs		-2808	-2892	-2979	-3068	-3160
Depreciation		-1000	-1600	-960	-576	-576
EBIT		152	-210	693	1365	1681
Taxes		-38	52	-173	-341	-420
NOPAT		114	-157	520	1024	1261
Depreciation Add Back		1000	1600	960	576	576
Operating Cash Flow		1114	1443	1480	1600	1837
Net Operating Working Capital						
Working Capital based on Rev		958	1036	1120	1212	0
Cash flow due to NOWC	-885.6	-72	-78	-84	-91	1212
Salvage Value						
Salvage Cashflow						1000
Book value of asset						288
gain or loss on sale						712
taxes on gain or loss on sale						-178
Net cashflow on salvage						822
Net Cashflow	-5885.6	1042	1365	1395	1508	3870
	-5885.6	-4938	-3811	-2762	-1732	671

BIND = BCR, IRR, NPV, and DPB

XL   Name [   ]   Date [   ]

Cashflow   [Calc.]

Period 0	$ -5885.6	Period 0 must be negative
Period 1	$ 1042	WACC 10 %
Period 2	$ 1365	
Period 3	$ 1395	**BCR or PI** 1.11 X
Period 4	$ 1508	(Benefit Cost Ratio or Profitability Index)
Period 5	$ 3870	**IRR** 13.6 %
Period 6	$ 0	(Internal Rate of Return)
Period 7	$ 0	**NPV** $ 670.81
Period 8	$ 0	(Net Present Value)
Period 9	$ 0	**DPB** 4.72 yrs
Period 10	$ 0	(discounted payback)

Notes:_____
_____
_____
_____

Lesson 17 Exercises

17-1. Complete a Summary and a Cash, CBUD and BIND for The company your instructor selects making sure the price per share and the number of shares outstanding are as of the most recent fiscal year end consistent with the financial data entered into the form.

Lesson 18: Real Options

Purpose: To show students how to calculate a real option when a binomial approach is employed.

Application: Use the "Real" tool at www.businessallstars.com/calculator to analyze a real option situation where the user must decide the price of an option to delay a decision until better information is available.

REAL Options Analysis
Copyright © 2013 ACBA - All Rights Reserved
BusinessAllstars.com

XL   Name [   ]   Date [   ]

Calc.

Time Period	Cashflow Upside	Cashflow Downside			
Period 0	$ -5934.8	$ -5836.4	(Period 0 cashflow must be negative)		
Period 1	$ 1203	$ 811			
Period 2	$ 1539	$ 1191	WACC	10	%
Period 3	$ 1583	$ 1207	Upside probability	50	%
Period 4	$ 1712	$ 1305	Months to decision	12	
Period 5	$ 4163	$ 3577	**Best NPV times Prob. Discounted**		
Period 6	$ 0	$ 0			
Period 7	$ 0	$ 0			
Period 8	$ 0	$ 0	Upside NPV	$ 622.01	
Period 9	$ 0	$ 0	Downside NPV	$ 0	
Period 10	$ 0	$ 0			
			Maximized NPV	$ 622.01	
NPV	$ 1374.28	$ -95.62	Expected NPV	$ 639.33	
			Real Option Value	$ -17.32	

Notes:_____
_____
_____
_____

111

CBUD - Capital Budgeting Model

Assumptions

Initial depreciable investment:	5,000.00	Initial Non-Depr. Investment:			0
1st year units:	3800	Growth: 5.0%	5.0%	5.0%	5.0%
Sales price per unit:	6.00	Inflation Assumption:			3.0%
Variable cost per unit;	4.90	First Year Fixed Cost:			2808
Deprec (3,5,7,10,15 or 20):	5	20.0% 32.0%	19.2%	11.5%	11.5%
Tax Rate:	25.0%	Salvage Value:			1000
NOIC chng. % of Revenue:	4.1%	Weighted Avg Cost of Capital:			10.0%

BCR	1.23	**IRR**	17.1%	**NPV**	1375	**DPB**	4.47	

	0	1	2	3	4	5
Initial Investment	-5000					
Units Sold		3800	3990	4190	4399	4619
Revenue		22800	24658	26668	28841	31192
Variable Costs		-18620	-20138	-21779	-23554	-25473
Fixed Costs		-2808	-2892	-2979	-3068	-3160
Depreciation		-1000	-1600	-960	-576	-576
EBIT		372	28	950	1643	1982
Taxes		-93	-7	-238	-411	-496
NOPAT		279	21	713	1232	1487
Depreciation Add Back		1000	1600	960	576	576
Operating Cash Flow		1279	1621	1673	1808	2063
Net Operating Working Capital						
Working Capital based on Rev		1011	1093	1182	1279	0
Cash flow due to NOWC	-934.8	-76	-82	-89	-96	1279
Salvage Value						
Salvage Cashflow						1000
Book value of asset						288
gain or loss on sale						712
taxes on gain or loss on sale						-178
Net cashflow on salvage						822
Net Cashflow	-5934.8	1203	1539	1583	1712	4163
	-5934.8	-4841	-3569	-2380	-1210	1375

CBUD - Capital Budgeting Model

Assumptions

Initial depreciable investment:	5,000.00	Initial Non-Depr. Investment:			0
1st year units:	3400	Growth: 5.0%	5.0%	5.0%	5.0%
Sales price per unit:	6.00	Inflation Assumption:			3.0%
Variable cost per unit;	4.90	First Year Fixed Cost:			2808
Deprec (3,5,7,10,15 or 20):	5	20.0% 32.0%	19.2%	11.5%	11.5%
Tax Rate:	25.0%	Salvage Value:			1000
NOIC chng. % of Revenue:	4.1%	Weighted Avg Cost of Capital:			10.0%

BCR	0.99	IRR	9.8%	NPV	(32)	DPB	

	0	1	2	3	4	5
Initial Investment	-5000					
Units Sold		3400	3570	3749	3936	4133
Revenue		20400	22063	23861	25805	27908
Variable Costs		-16660	-18018	-19486	-21074	-22792
Fixed Costs		-2808	-2892	-2979	-3068	-3160
Depreciation		-1000	-1600	-960	-576	-576
EBIT		-68	-447	435	1087	1380
Taxes		17	112	-109	-272	-345
NOPAT		-51	-336	327	815	1035
Depreciation Add Back		1000	1600	960	576	576
Operating Cash Flow		949	1264	1287	1391	1611
Net Operating Working Capital						
Working Capital based on Rev		905	978	1058	1144	0
Cash flow due to NOWC	-836.4	-68	-74	-80	-86	1144
Salvage Value						
Salvage Cashflow						1000
Book value of asset						288
gain or loss on sale						712
taxes on gain or loss on sale						-178
Net cashflow on salvage						822
Net Cashflow	-5836.4	881	1191	1207	1305	3577
	-5836.4	-5036	-4052	-3145	-2254	-32

REAL Options Analysis

XL Name [   ] Date [   ]

Time Period	Cashflow Upside	Cashflow Downside		
Period 0	$ -5934.8	$ -5836.4	(Period 0 cashflow must be negative)	
Period 1	$ 1203	$ 811		
Period 2	$ 1539	$ 1191	WACC	10 %
Period 3	$ 1583	$ 1207	Upside probability	25 %
Period 4	$ 1712	$ 1305	Months to decision	12
Period 5	$ 4163	$ 3577		**Best NPV times Prob. Discounted**
Period 6	$ 0	$ 0		
Period 7	$ 0	$ 0		
Period 8	$ 0	$ 0	Upside NPV	$ 311
Period 9	$ 0	$ 0	Downside NPV	$ 0
Period 10	$ 0	$ 0		
			Maximized NPV	$ 311
NPV	$ 1374.28	$ -95.62	Expected NPV	$ 271.86
			Real Option Value	$ 39.14

Calc.

Notes:_____
_____
_____
_____

Lesson 18 Exercises

18-1. Complete a VERN model for the company your instructor selects making sure the price per share and the number of shares outstanding are as of the most recent fiscal year end consistent with the financial data entered into the form.

18-2. Complete a VERN model for a public company that you have selected as the entity you intend to analyze throughout the rest of this course. Make sure the price per share and the number of shares outstanding is as of the most recent fiscal year end consistent with the financial data entered into the form.

Lesson 19: Finance Theory

Purpose: Learn general finance concepts and how various finance activities can be categorized into financing, investing, and operating decisions. Also, show how the sum of all the parts leads to the valuation decision.

Application: Use the "." found at www.businessallstars.com/calculator to access a series of diagrams showing a graphical representation of the balance sheet and income statement. The sequence begins with financing, proceeds through investing in long-term assets that will be used to generate the operating activity of the business. Receiving revenue and paying expenses result in increases in short-term assets and liabilities. The entity in total is then analyzed to determine its value.

Calculator   Next

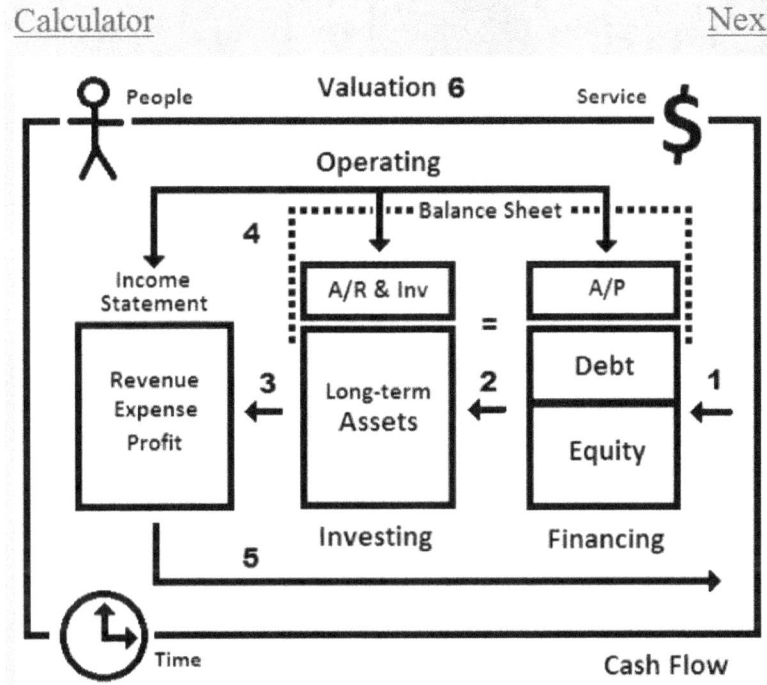

The Financial Map

THE GLOBAL CONCEPT of FINANCE:

Value today equals all future cash flows discounted to the present.

The Critical Question:

Does the entity have the people who can deliver a valued service over time that will result in a positive cash flow?

Several Principles to keep in mind.

1. Measure in cash flow.
2. Decisions are made in today's dollars.
3. The discount rate is the cost of financing.
4. Cost for a company is return for a financier.
5. The "time lag" principle states that investment comes at the beginning and return comes at the end.

Notes:_____

_____

_____

_____

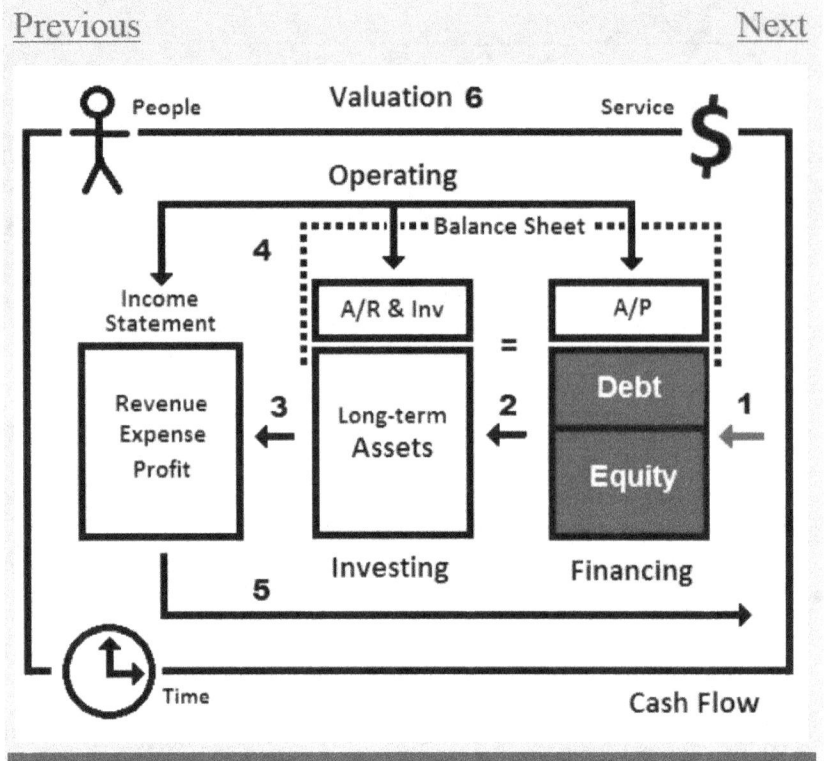

2. Financing Activity

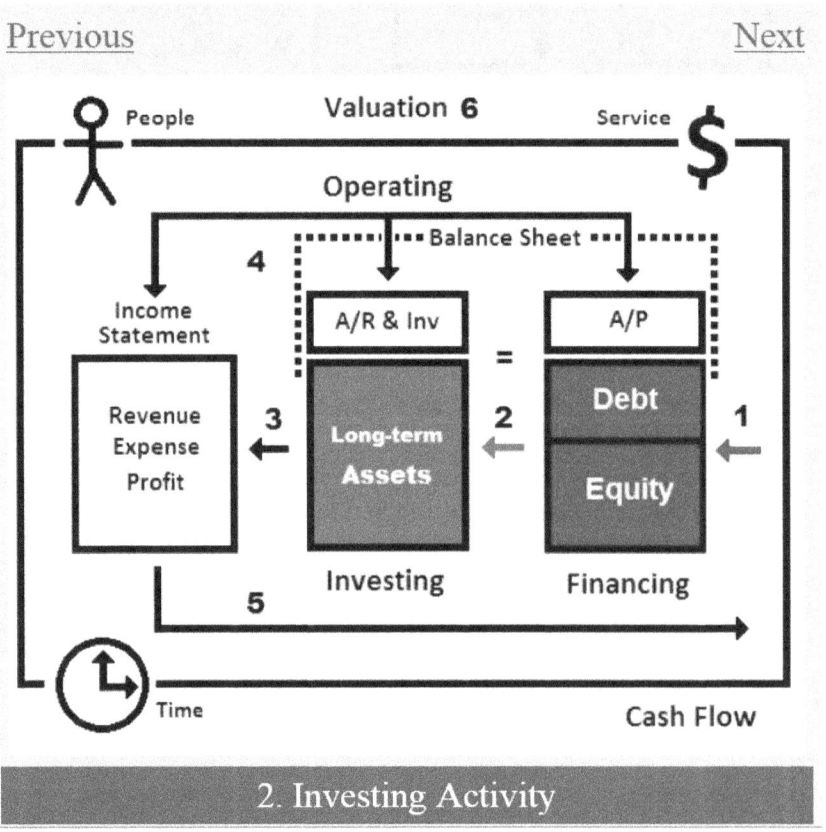

2. Investing Activity

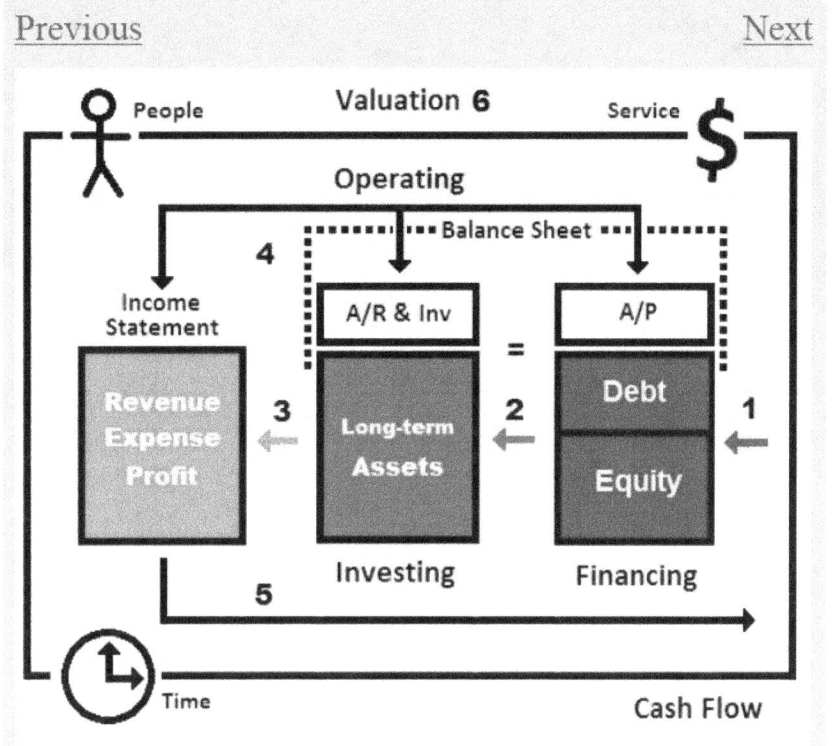

3. Operating Activity

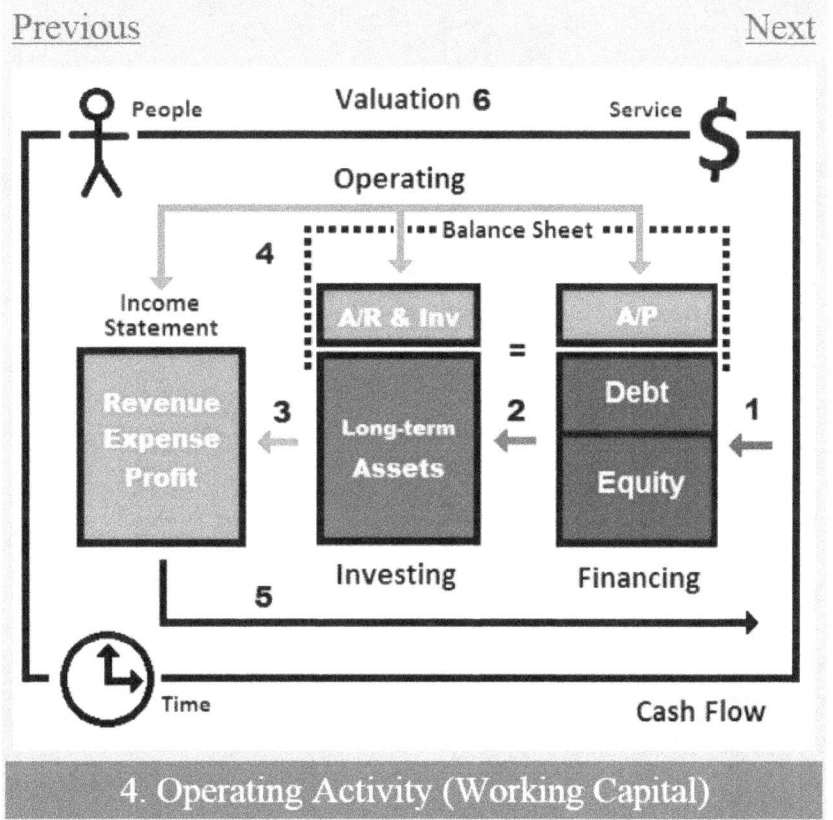

4. Operating Activity (Working Capital)

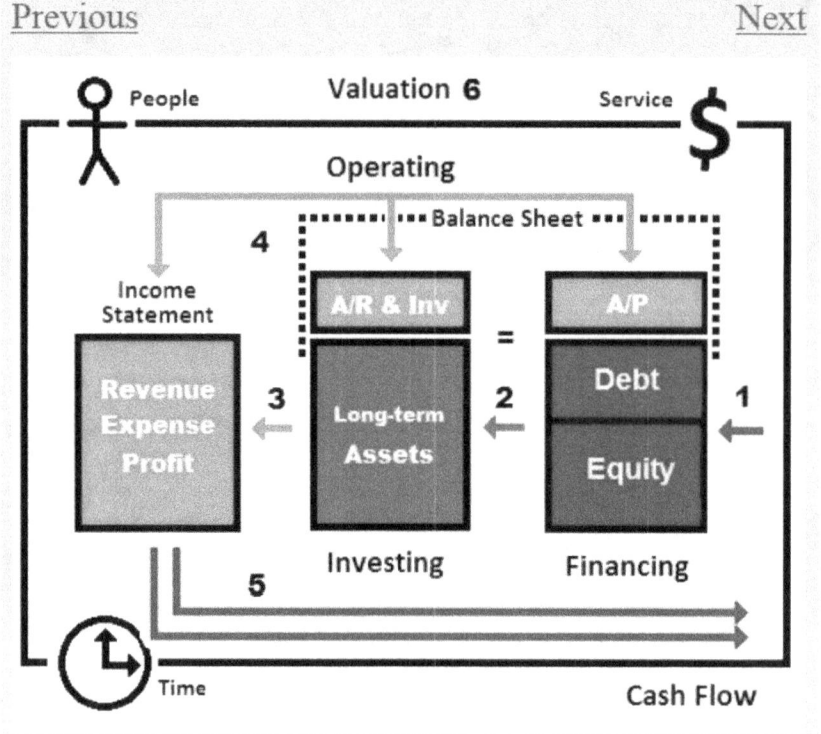

5. Financing Activity (Cost of Capital)

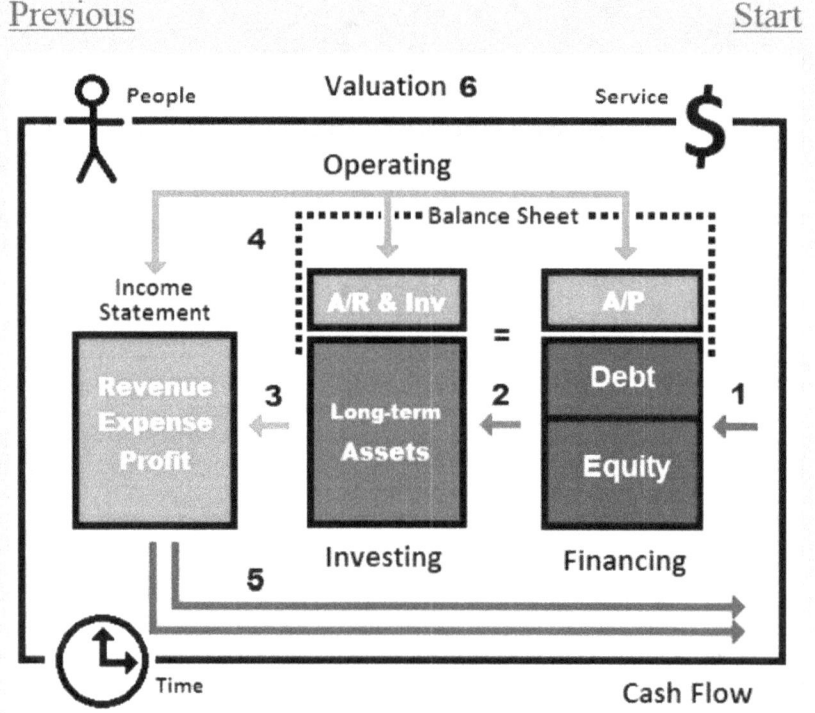

6. Valuation Activity

19-1.

MAP (Matching)

Name _____

	Fill each Box with a single Letter representing an Answer from the list at right	**Answers**
1.	Receiving credit from vendors	F = Financing
2.	Purchasing Fixed Assets	I = Investing
3.	Acquiring Inventory	O = Operating
4.	Extending credit to customers	V = Valuation
5.	Borrow from a Bank	
6.	Incure Expenses	
7.	Paying salaries and wages	
8.	Set the budgeted revenue	
9.	Set the capital budget	
10.	Selling common stock	
11.	Calculate the Price to Earnings ratio	
12.	Calculate the net income	
13.	Paying a dividend	
14.	Determine the cost of capital	
15.	Find the free cash flow value	

Lesson 20: Dissecting Revenue (VERN)

Purpose: To show students how to analyze the change in revenue from one year to the next to break out variances due to volume, efficiency, and rate.

Application: Use the "VERN" tool at www.businessallstars.com/calculator to dissect the revenue from one year to the next. The user will click the "Revenue" button and then at the bottom of the page, enter the current year's revenue, prior year's revenue, current years Cost of goods sold (Cost of Revenue) and prior years Cost of goods sold. The inflation rate that was expected is enter in the bottom and the analysis will determine if there is any efficiency loss.

VERN-Variance Analysis
Copyright © 2013 ACBA - All Rights Reserved
BusinessAllstars.com

XL   Name Dollar General (DG)   Date 1/31/13   Calc.

	ACTUAL	BUDGET	
Units	10725	10109	● Revenue
Quantity per unit	0.9989	1	○ Direct Materials
Rate per quantity	1.4955	1.4647	○ Direct Labor
			○ Variable Overhead
			○ Fixed Overhead

Actual (AV x AQ) x AR	Standard (AV x AQ) x BR	Flexed (AU x BQ) x BR	Budget (BU x BQ) x BR
16022	15692	15709	14807
330 F	-17 U	902 F	1215 F
Revenue Rate Var.	Revenue Effic. Var.	Revenue Vol. Var.	Net Var.

	313 F	Total flexible budget revenue variance

	Enter Data below only for Revenue Calculations	
Current Yr Revenue	$ 16022	Prior Yr Revenue	$ 14807
Current Yr COGS	$ 10937	Prior Yr COGS	$ 10109
Inflation Rate year over year	2.1 %	

Notes:_____

_____

_____

_____

VERN-Variance Analysis

XL Name Family Dollar (FDO)   Date 8/24/12   Calc.

	ACTUAL	**BUDGET**	
			◉ Revenue
Units	1890	1595	○ Direct Materials
Quantity per unit	0.9876	1	○ Direct Labor
Rate per quantity	1.5504	1.5185	○ Variable Overhead
			○ Fixed Overhead

Actual (AV x AQ) x AR	Standard (AV x AQ) x BR	Flexed (AU x BQ) x BR	Budget (BU x BQ) x BR
2894	2834	2870	2422
60 F	-36 U	448 F	472 F
Revenue Rate Var.	Revenue Effic. Var.	Revenue Vol. Var.	Net Var.

24	F	Total flexible budget revenue variance

	Enter Data below only for Revenue Calculations	
Current Yr Revenue	$ 2894	Prior Yr Revenue	$ 2422
Current Yr COGS	$ 1923	Prior Yr COGS	$ 1595
Inflation Rate year over year		2.1 %	

Table of Inflation Rates by Month and Year (1999-2013)

Year	Jan	Feb	Mar	Apr	May	Jun	Jul	Aug	Sep	Oct	Nov	Dec	Ave
2013	1.6	2.0	1.5	1.1	1.4								
2012	2.9	2.9	2.7	2.3	1.7	1.7	1.4	1.7	2.0	2.2	1.8	1.7	2.1
2011	1.6	2.1	2.7	3.2	3.6	3.6	3.6	3.8	3.9	3.5	3.4	3.0	3.2

http://www.usinflationcalculator.com/inflation/current-inflation-rates/

Lesson 20 Exercises

20-1. Complete a VERN analysis a company your instructor selects using real data from the current and prior year's revenues and cost of revenue. Use an inflation assumption that is consistent with those used in the workbook.

20-2. Complete a VERN analysis for a public company that you have selected as the entity you intend to analyze throughout the rest of this course using real data from the current and prior year's revenues and cost of revenue. Use an inflation assumption that is consistent with those used in the workbook.

Lesson 21: Cost Flow

Purpose: To show students how costs flow within a company.

Application: Use the "COST" tool at www.businessallstars.com/calculator to show the cost flow system within a company.

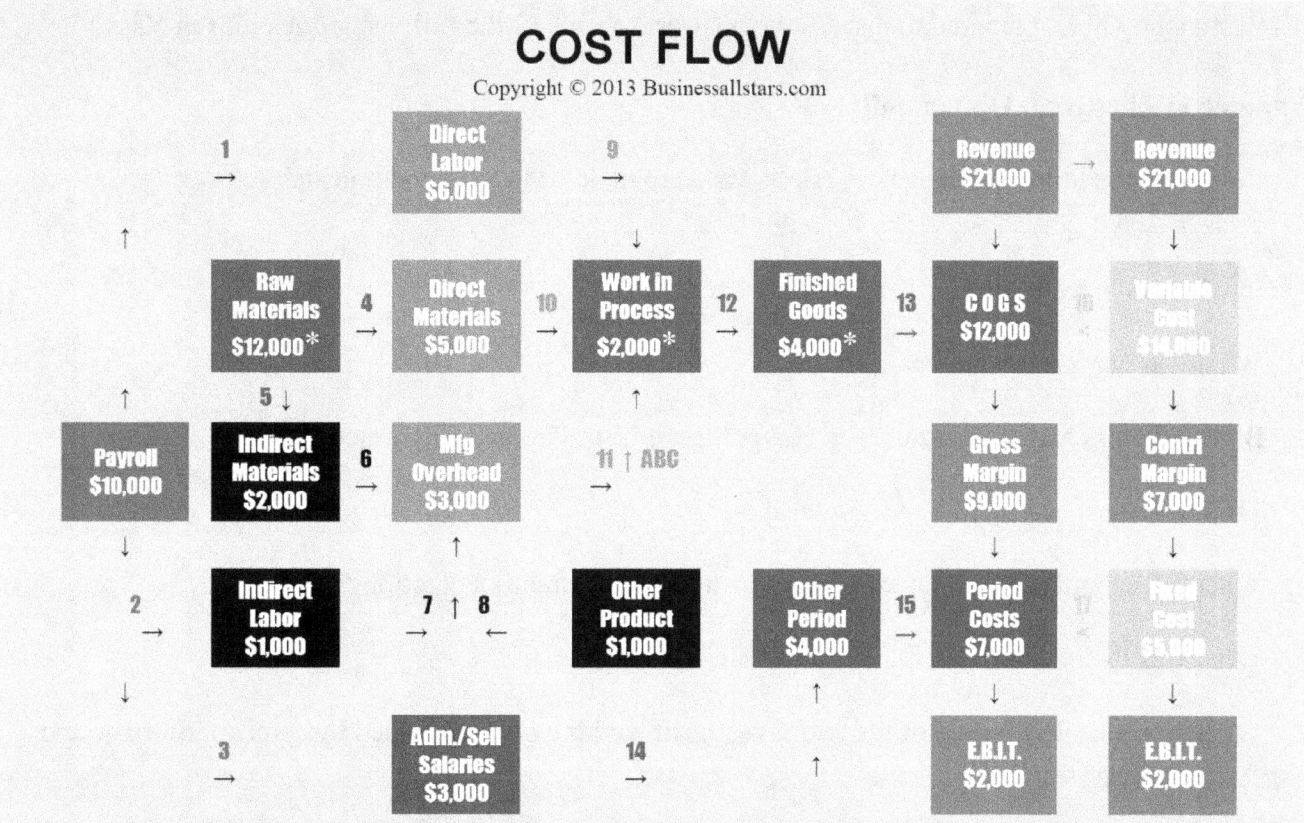

1, 2 & 3: Payroll is divided into Product Costs (Direct & Indirect Labor) and Period Costs (Admin & Selling Salaries).

4 & 5: Applied Raw Materials are divided into Product Costs for Direct and Indirect Materials.

6, 7 & 8: Indirect Materials, Indirect Labor and Other Products Costs are accumulated in the Manufacturing Overhead Account.

9, 10 & 11: Direct Labor, Direct Materials and Manufacturing Overhead are assigned to individual jobs in the Work-in-Process.

 [NOTE]: ABC or Activity Based Costing is a process of allocating Manufacturing Overhead to jobs based on various activities.

12: Jobs that are completed are transfered out of Work-In-Process to the Finished Goods inventory.

13: Finished Goods that are sold leave inventory and are accounted for as Cost of Goods Sold on the Income Statement.

14 & 15: Administrative & Selling Salaries along with Other Period Costs are expensed as Period Costs on the Income Statement.

16 & 17: Costs of Goods Sold and Period Costs are divided into either Variable or Fixed Costs on the Contribution Statement.

 [NOTE]: Boxes with yellow lettering are generated from outside the system.

 [NOTE]: * designates a beginning inventory number.

Beginning + Added - Ending = Subtracted

Appendix A: My Years with General Motors [Part 1]

Purpose: To demonstrate how an entrepreneur building a company from the ground up needs to be ever conscious of the importance financial aspects.

by Alfred P. Sloan, Jr.
Questions from Reading Selected Chapters
(Each student will be prepared to discuss the answers to each of the following questions in class.)

Chapter 1: The Great Opportunity – 1

1. Complete the following sentence: "Both Mr. Durant and Mr. ford had unusual _____, _____, _____, _____, and _____."

2. In what ways were Mr. Ford and Mr. Durant different?

3. What was Mr. Durant's weakness?

4. Between 1908 and 1910 how many companies did Mr. Durant bring together?

5. Mr. Durant expected economies in what areas?

6. What three simultaneous patterns emerged from Mr. Durant's operations?

7. What was the result of Mr. Durant's wheeler-dealing?

8. What was the significance of the two investment banking groups headed by James J. Storrow and Albert Strauss in 1910?

9. Who was president of General Motors in 1915 and what was his contribution?\

10. Who became head of the Buick division in 1912?

11. What stunning event happened in 1915 regarding the stockholders?

12. What car company was created in 1911 that would have an impact on GM?

13. How did du Pont come to be involved with GM?

14. How did Mr. Durant regain control in 1916?

15. What happened to Mr. Nash?

16. What were the five points in favor of the investment in GM summarized by Mr. Raskob?

17. What percent of GM did du Pont own as of 1917?

18. What became du Pont's roll in GM?

19. GM acquired what car company in 1918?

20. Complete this sentence: "On occasion, when out in the field, he would make _____ _____ to get something started, and this sometimes caused _____ _____ in the general office."

21. What caused "the crisis from which the modern General Motors Corporation would emerge?"

Chapter 2: The Great Opportunity – II

1. Complete the following sentence: "I think we have all had in common a capability for being _____ to our respective interests."

2. How did Sloan come to be the general manager of the Hyatt Roller Bearing Company?

3. Complete the following: "It was difficult to get _____, and when we got it and _____, we needed _____ _____ that we could not get outside the company."

4. Complete the following: "Our _____ became so good that it got to be a question of how rapidly we could expand our _____, with new _____, new machinery, new _____, and the like, to keep up with the rapidly expanding _____ business."

5. Who was responsible for bringing the technique of interchangeable parts into automobile manufacturing?

6. How did Sloan get to be an executive at General Motors?

7. When Sloan and Chrysler were rival heads of car companies what did they use to do together?

8. Sloan says that he found Mr. Durant, a very persuasive man and what else?

9. What were the three reasons that selling Hyatt's business to General Motors seemed like a good idea?

10. Sloan wanted how much for his company and eventually settled for how much?

11. What was United Motors?

12. Complete the following: "One day in 1919 I went in and told him that I thought that, in view of the large public interest in the corporation's shares, we should have an _____ ____ by a _____ _____ _____."

13. Complete the following: "As to _____, we did not have adequate k_____ or _____ of the individual _____ _____."

14. Complete the following: "It was a case of _____ among the _____ for available _____ and of different _____ at the top."

15. Did the corporation have a philosophy of cutting requests or raising more funds to meet demands?

16. Complete the following: "An effort was made to raise $_____, but only $_____ was realized. This was the first signal from the outside financial environment that the corporation was ____ _____ ____ _____..."

17. Complete the following "_____ followed the same runaway course as the overruns on _____ _____."

18. In September of 1920 what happened to the automobile market in America?

19. What happened to Mr. Durrant in November of 1920?

Appendix B: My Years with General Motors [Part 2]

Purpose: To show students how financial controls are critical to the success of a growing business and how demands from capital appropriations, inventory build-up and earnings management are critical.

by Alfred P. Sloan, Jr.

Questions from Reading Selected Chapters

(Each student will be prepared to discuss the answers to each of the following questions in class.)

Chapter 8: the Development of Financial Controls

1. Who originally developed the DuPont Model of emphasizing capital turnover as well as profit margin in calculating ROI?

2. Who initiated the technique of displaying charts of the efficiency of divisional performance at general managers' meetings at DuPont?

3. Who, and in what year, made an effort to apply the principle of ROI in appropriating funds to the operating side of the corporation at General Motors?

4. During the expansion of 1919 three problems emerged that resulted in the crisis of 1920, what were they?

5. What was the financial model that is one fot he chief bases for strategic business decisions?

6. The story of how General Motors survived the crisis of 1920 falls into two parts. What are they?

7. Summarize the four principles that were to be satisfied in appropriations procedures.

8. Under the new proposals could general managers authorize expenditures?

9. How often were reports of construction in progress to be made?

10. Each appropriation request was to receive consideration and analysis from whom before a commitment was made?

11. What would you say about information on appropriations requests?

12. Why was General Motors short of cash in 1920?

13. Initially, what level in the corporation controlled cash?

14. Under the consolidated cash-control system explain how each of the following worked: Depository accounts; minimum and maximum balances; transfer by telegraph; and settlement certificates.

15. The corporation began calculating a month ahead what their cash would be for what time period?

16. What components were considered in the month ahead cash calculation?

17. What did the company do with the excess cash their cash plan generated?

18. What did the Inventory Committee do?

19. General Managers submitted a monthly budget to the Inventory Committee which showed estimated sales for how many months?

20. Inventory levels and inventory turnover changed by how much between Sep. 1920 and Jun 1922?

21. What attitude did the company take toward expectations of increased future sales?

22. Eventually, what became the key and long-term solution to inventory control in the company?

23. The scope of the four-month forecast was eventually enlarged to include what components?

24. The enlarged forecasts were to be in the hands of the V.P. by what date?

25. What was the key element in the forecast?

26. How often were division managers required to report on actual unit production and sales at the factory?

27. At the end of each month division managers had to report to the V.P. what three statistics?

28. Where was the big gap in the information system at headquarters?

29. Beginning in 1922 the division managers had to submit year end estimates of what three statistics for what three conditions?

30. Complete the following sentence: "There will always be some conflict between the _____ and the _____, since the _____ naturally think they can do something about a statistical situation, as they often can."

31. Complete the following sentence: "It is not often that the _____ of a large corporation himself discovers visible overproduction by a _____ of the inventory."

32. Complete the following sentence: "The _____ in this instance was right and the _____ were wrong. Everywhere the _____ were excessive."

33. Because of the excessive inventory of 1924 Sloan developed a procedure called the "Monthly Forecast----" of what?

34. There had to be a reconciliation of what two types of people to reconcile production levels with seasonal peaks in sales?

35. The basic problem of controlling production was determined to eventually involve what two actions?

36. The corporate-wide estimate of sales was based upon what two components?

37. What is the "index volume?"

38. A system of statistical reports to be sent by dealers was worked out in 1924/25. What was in these reports and how often were they sent?

39. What were a "pyramid of demand" and the so-called "saturation point?"

40. The 1923 study failed to gauge accurately the future growth of the market largely because it underestimated the effect of what two important factors on new car sales?

41. Complete the following: "Since considerations of economical _____ and economical _____ were thus diametrically opposed, planning and judgment were required to find a _____."

42. How was the solution to the previously mentioned problem addressed?

43. How did the production schedule respond to the actual trend of retail demand?

44. The objectivity and systematic use of retail demand and production schedules operated as a basic control on what other financial controls?

45. The basic elements of financial control in General Motors are what four items?

46. Explain the concept of "the economic return attainable."

47. Complete the following: "The _____ thus established were compared with _____. The heart of financial-control principles lies in such comparisons."

48. What was in Sloan's "little black book" he carried around on his visits to divisions?

49. Uniformity was essential to financial control. How did this affect the accounting practices?

50. Explain the "principle of dual responsibility" for divisional comptrollers.

Appendix C: My Years with General Motors [Part 3]

Purpose: To show students how financial aspects of a corporation extend into the areas of raising capital, innovative approaches to extending customer financing and employee incentives.

by Alfred P. Sloan, Jr.

Questions from Reading Selected Chapters

(Each student will be prepared to discuss the answers to each of the following questions in class.)

Chapter 11: Financial Growth

1. Complete the following: "Of necessity, during _____ and _____, this has meant that dividends have been something less than average. The shareholders thus assumed the risk of building for future with no certainty of _____."

2. Sloan identifies three periods of corporate existence, from a financial standpoint. What were they?

3. Relative to expansion the 1920 annual report reflected what strategic position that was: "unwise to undertake the production of materials that do not _____."

4. Complete the following: "so rapid a growth could not have been financed entirely _____."

5. Complete the following: "most of the expenditures were made in _____, and so the corporation had to go to _____."

6. In 1919 the company attempted to put together a syndicate to raise $50,000,000 but only raised how much? What does it mean by syndicate?

7. Why did the 1920 issue of securities fail?

8. What does Capital employed mean?

9. What does New Working Capital represent?

10. By the end of 1922 bank debt was liquidated and assets conservatively valued. At what capacity did the company operate? Was this a good move?

11. Compare the capital expenditures of the two periods 1918-20 and 1923-25. Was this consistency and inconsistency good strategically and/or tactically?

12. What European car companies were acquired in 1925 and 1929? Assess these strategic moves.

13. Complete the following: "Thanks to the _____ and _____ controls, we were able to finance virtually this entire expansion program out of _____ and _____ and still pay out almost two-thirds of _____ to shareholders?

14. During the depression, how many years did the company fail to earn a profit or pay a dividend?

15. Do you agree with the dividend policy during the depression?

16. Complete the following: "I think the story I have told shows that we had simply _____. This was perhaps the greatest payoff of our system of _____ and _____ controls.

17. Complete the following: "As a result of the speed with which we acted when sales began to fail, we were able to _____ in line with the sales decline and to _____ so that operations remained profitable.

18. Complete the following: "Our sales declined _____ percent, from _____ million in 1929 to only _____ million in 1932.

19. What would justify the dividend payout in 1932?

20. What adversely affected earnings in 1937?

21. What produces a very rapid obsolescence of productive facilities in the automotive industry?

22. By 1935 the corporation gave consideration to three special factors affecting capacity. What were they?

23. What percentage of earnings was paid in dividends between 1930-39?

24. In the 1930s how did capital expenditures compare with provision for depreciation?

25. Complete the following: "The strategic question in industrial finance, assuming you have something to work with in the way of a going business, is how to _____."

26. Complete the following: "in principle, _____ enhances the return on the stockholders' investment, while at the same time increasing the _____ involved."

27. Between 1921 and 1946 what was the corporations policy toward long-term debt?

28. "The Challenge" recognized that an urgent need would exist, when the war ended, to convert plants from war to peace production as quickly as possible in order to do what three things?

29. What three areas were addressed in the long-term studies that projected the company's position for five to ten years?

30. In 1946 were dividends greater or less than earnings? By how much?

31. Who did the company look to for long-term borrowing in mid-1946?

32. Why was the preferred-stock issue of 1946 attractive?

33. Complete the following: "We had learned from experience that wars create a _____."

34. What is wrong with this statement: "it was clear that we would have to raise new capital if we were to continue to pay out a substantial part of each year's earnings in the form of dividends."

35. The stock offering of 1955 required the underwriters to subscribe to what percent of the issue.?"

36. The market price of General Motors stock, rose from how much in 1945 to what level in 1962?

37. Complete the following: "The measure of the worth of a business enterprise as a business, however, is not merely _____ or _____ but _____ since it is their capital that is being risked and it is in their interests first of all that the corporation is supposed to be run in the private-enterprise scheme of things?

38. Identify two things of interest in the charts showing General Motors historical data.

39. Complete the following: "Due to the _____ and through a _____, the units of industry have become larger and larger. This is because of the continuously _____ for industry's products and services resulting from the production of _____ at _____. There is superimposed upon this evolutionary process the additional influence of an increasing integration of manufacturing processes involved in mass production. The effect of such an evolution on the capital structure is to require ever increasing _____."

40. Complete the following: "Our performance has been demonstrated day by day in our production and distribution of _____."

Chapter 17: GMAC

1. GMAC was in competition with what four other types of financial institutions?

2. What does Sloan mean by "closed business"?

3. What is the difference between retail and wholesale credit?

4. What created the need for a broad approach to consumer financing?

5. If people had to pay for large purchases in cash, what would be the impact on the economy, i.e. jobs, production, and sales?

6. Complete the following: "Bankers…thought of the automobile as a _____ and a _____, and not as the greatest revolution in transportation since the railway."

7. Complete the following: "[Bankers] believing apparently that whatever fostered _____ must discourage _____."

8. Complete the following: "As the business grew and manufacturers continued to require cash on delivery, dealers simply did not have funds to finance _____, not to mention _____."

9. At the time the book was written what percent of all automobile retail sales in the United States were on installment plans?

10. From the period of 1919 to 1933 what was the maximum loss ratio for automobile sales financed through installment loans?

11. What is meant by "trust receipts or other security documents?"

12. Between 1919 and 1963 did GMAC finance the sale of more new or used cars?

13. If a sale is financed through GMAC, does the dealer or GMAC undertake collection of payments from the customer?

14. In the beginning, what were the two primary motives for GM starting GMAC?

15. The risks in consumer financing centered around what three problems?

16. Because of the risks in consumer financing the company relies on what four factors supporting the extension of credit?

17. Complete the following: "Installment credit, he said, nor only strengthens the motive to _____ but increases the individual's _____." Do you believe this?

18. What effect does installment credit have on purchasing power and production?

19. How did GMAC deal with the possibilities of loss collateral (the care itself)?

20. Why was General Exchange Insurance Corporation needed?

21. Is GMAC a "nonrecourse system" or not?

22. What was the "6% plan" offered by GMAC?

23. Why did the federal government go after GMAC?

24. What were the major contributions of GMAC to GM, consumers, and society?

Chapter 22: Incentive Compensation

1. General Motors, in 1942 gave what justification for a bonus plan?

2. Is there any relationship between a bonus plan and decentralization?

3. Complete the following: "the interests of the _____ and _____ are best served by making _____ partners in the corporation's prosperity, and that each individual should be rewarded in proportion to his contribution to the profit of _____ and of _____."

4. What modification to the incentive plan occurred in 1957?

5. What does the "6 per cent" limit indicate?

6. What is the maximum that can be paid out?

7. Is the bonus plan a profit-sharing plan? Why or why not?

8. What is the benefit derived by paying a bonus in stock?

9. Complete the following: "it provided for bonuses to be paid to employees 'who have contributed to its [General Motors] success in a special degree by their _____, _____, _____, _____, or _____."

10. How were employees determined to be eligible for bonuses?

11. What was the "Manager's Securities Company?"

12. Was the "Manager's Security Company" concept sound?

13. What were the two reasons Du Pont put up stock in the MSC?

Appendix D: Managing [Part 1]

Purpose: To show students how to manage a business with financial accountability and a determination to focus on sustainability.

by Harold Geneen, with Alvin Moscow
Questions from Reading Selected Chapters
(Each student will be prepared to discuss the answers to each of the following questions in class.)

Introduction

1. How many consecutive quarters did ITT increase its earnings over the year before?

2. Complete the following: "Decide what it is you _____ ___ ___, and then start doing it."

3. Complete the following: "Geneen ran ITT with tight, _____ ____ _____, a large headquarters staff to _____ ___ _____, and, above all, _____-__-_____ _____ with the managers of ITT's profit centers worldwide."

4. Complete the following: "He went over the major problems of each company, which were '___-_____' in the monthly reports. But he also looked for _____ because he believed all large corporations, like ITT, were _____."

5. Complete the following: "Geneen's _____ _____ for answers in an open forum was Socratic. One question led to another. He demanded _____ and _____ backed by _____."

Chapter 1: Theory G on Management

1. Are management theories reliable?

2. How did most successful managerial run their businesses?

3. Complete the following: "___ _____ is one of the worst traps devised to ensnare the successful businessman."

4. Complete the following: "Not only would such a formula not work, it would violate everything we had built up in twenty years at ITT, which was the _____ in ___-____ management, all _____ _____ as fast as possible toward a single, _____-_____ set of goals."

5. Complete the following: "The only way I knew how to judge people at ITT was by the _____ ___ _____."

6. Complete the following: "The simple truth is that business is _____ _ _____. It follows ___ _____ ____; nor is it as predictable as machines."

7. Complete the following: "But a _____ _____ is probably most important as a means of gathering in facts."

8. Complete the following: "We learned as we went along: our bank of _____ grew richer; we become _____ and more _____ in handling more complex problems; we became more self-confident of our _____."

9. What does it mean "You keep your eye on the pot?"

Chapter 2: How to Run a Business

1. Complete the following: "When all is said and done, a company, its chief executive, and his whole management team are judged by one criterion along---_____."

2. What did Geneen do at Raytheon? How did it perform?

3. Complete the following: "I came to ITT knowing perhaps _____ ___ _____ about the company, for what I had read and been old about ITT turned out to be largely _____."

4. How did Geneen prepare himself to be comptroller at Bell & Howell in Chicago?

5. Detail what did Geneen did "the first week or so" to prepare himself to assume the CEO responsibilities at ITT?

6. How did the European operations function relative to the leadership of Hank Scudder?

7. How did the European subsidiaries operate, before Geneen, relative to each other?

8. Complete the following: "I had long believed that the primary role of a chief executive was to serve as a management team's _____ and show his team where the _____ were and how best to _____ ____, and finally to lead the way _____ __ _____."

9. What targets did Geneen set for ITT?

10. What did Geneen mean by "quality of earnings?"

11. Complete the following: "…I needed to attract to ITT the very best corporate managers and staff. I wanted men who not only were professionally capable and competent but also had the inner drive to thrive on the ____ _____, _____ _____, and _____ thinking necessary to accomplish my idea of a bottom line."

12. Complete the following: "So, early on, I decided that if I and my headquarters team intended to monitor and oversee the European operations, I owed it to the European managers to __ ____ ___ ___ _____."

13. Why did Geneen eliminate long-range planning?

Chapter 3: Experience and Cash

Summarize the historical experience and background of Harold Geneen.

Appendix E: Managing [Part 2]

Purpose: To show students how finance involves reporting systems and how various cultures can be uniformly merged into a successful whole.

by Harold Geneen, with Alvin Moscow
Questions from Reading Selected Chapters
(Each student will be prepared to discuss the answers to each of the following questions in class.)

Chapter 4: Two Organizational Structures

1. Complete the following: "What happened then? Word gets around that if you fail, you get fired. So men, who would not have otherwise, begin to _____ ___ __ _____."

2. Describe the policy of any staff man could go anywhere in the company and ask any kind of questions.

3. The comptrollers in each and every division had to submit their financial reports where?

4. Complete the following: "Management manages by making decisions and by seeing that those decisions are implemented. And the only way management can do that successfully is to have ___ _____ to the _____ of any situation affecting the _____ of the company."

5. Complete the following: "…it is only by knowing the realities of ___ ___ _____ and the realities of the _____ the management can hope to manage satisfactorily."

6. Explain the monthly reporting system that Geneen put into place.

7. Complete the following: "…the best answer was always the same: We had to _____ _____. That meant, of course, better and better _____ and better and better group _____."

8. Are functions or people more important?

9. Describe the monthly meetings.

10. Complete the following: "The look in a man's face, his ___ __ ____, his ___ _____ made a difference in the decisions I was making."

11. Complete the following: "Oftentimes, as we explored a situation, we found that the reason for a problem was _____ __ _____, but something _____ _____."

12. What did "no surprises" mean?

13. What did the "red flag page" accomplish?

14. How should a person handle mistakes?

15. What did Geneen mean by "imaginative and creative."

16. Complete the following: "The highest art of professional management requires the literal ability to _____ a ___ ____ from all others."

17. What is an unshakable fact?

18. Complete the following: "The only way a subsidiary company manager could prepare himself for a General Managers Meeting was to demand of his own people that they ___ ___ ____of _____ going on in their company."

19. How did Geneen get an idea of a manager's capabilities?

20. Were people afraid to talk?

21. How long were the GMM meetings?

22. What were the weeks of time commitment to GMM meetings during a year?

Chapter 5: Management Must Manage

1. Why did they hold General Manager Meeting?

2. Complete the following: "It meant that we would do everything we had to do (that was _____ and _____) to bring in the _____ we desired."

3. Good planning must include what steps?

4. Complete the following: "The truth is that the so-called 'facts' are almost always colored by the bias of the man presenting them. So you might do well to get your 'facts' from __ _____ __ _____."

5. How does a manager determine the reality of a situation?

6. Complete the following: "Management means making something happen, not ___ __ __ _____ while opportunities pass you by."

7. What is "the inverse ratio of time to veracity?"

8. What was Bud James "new, imaginative, and creative idea?"

9. Complete the following: "If you cannot solve the problem of your environment, change your _____."

Chapter 6: Leadership

1. What do you manage in a business?

2. What is leadership?

3. What is the single most important ingredient in the recipe for business success?

4. Complete the following: "Business could be a ____ _____, a ____ __ _____, something to look forward to everyday, and the rewards went much further than one's annual salary and bonuses."

5. What binds people in chains of insecurity?

6. What is "participatory leadership?"

7. What kind of people did Geneen target to hire?

8. What are a "rare breed?"

9. Complete the following: "...the most important element in establishing a happy, prosperous atmosphere was an insistence upon ____, ____, and _____ communications up and down the ranks of our management structure."

10. How did Geneen feel about criticism?

11. How did Geneen feel about office politics?

12. What kind of person should a company get rid of?

13. What was Geneen's thinking about imaginative thinking and good ideas?

14. Complete the following: "The important thing is not ___ is right, but _____ is right."

15. How many times can you double-cross a subordinate?

16. How is it to work for someone you respect and admire?

17. Complete the following: "The dedicated, _____ _____ of a chief executive is like a lifeline or a safety net to his management team and, in fact, to the whole company."

18. How did a subordinate gain the support of the CEO?

19. Complete the following: "A chief executive who has conquered his ____ ___ _____ listens to such criticism, for even if it is wrong, he will probably learn something."

20. What did Geneen think about "scaring the hell" out of your subordinates?

21. Complete the following: "But I am convinced that _____ is the single most important ingredient in business management, and that those attitudes of the chief executive which inspire his people to _____ and to _____ contribute as much as ___ to ___ _____ of a company's success."

Appendix F: Managing [Part 3]

Purpose: To show students how the detail of the numbers is critical and that early warning systems protect the consistent deployment of resources for success.

by Harold Geneen, with Alvin Moscow

Questions from Reading Selected Chapters

(Each student will be prepared to discuss the answers to each of the following questions in class.)

Chapter 7: The Cluttered---Desk Executive

1. What does Geneen mean by momentum in meetings?

2. What is the most important factor in an acquisition?

Chapter 8: Not Alcoholism---Egotism

What are the key concepts presented in this chapter?

Chapter 9: The Numbers

1. Complete the following: "When I read ssets of numbers, either vertically or horizontally, I automatically translate them into meaningful _____ _____."

2. What causes Geneen to look behind the numbers?

3. If the "numbers are not the business" what are they?

4. Complete the following: "Once you start digging into the areas which the numbers represent, then you get into the _____ of your business."

5. Complete the following: "You don't want to manage the _____; you don't want to push sales or receivables from one quarter to another, for the ____ will always catch up with you."

6. Complete the following: "…the difference between well-managed companies and not-so-well-managed companies is the ____ __ _____ they pay to _____, the temperature chart of their business. How often are the numbers reported up the ____ __ _____? How _____ are those numbers? How much variation is tolerated between _____ _____ and _____ _____? How soon is attention directed to and action taken on _____ deemed significant? How deep does management dig for its answer?"

7. Describe the "early warnings system" and "no surprises."

8. The quality of the numbers depends on who?

9. Why is managing a company like "writing in the snow."

10. What happens when a manager finds gaps in the information that he needs?"

11. Complete the following: "To sit back and wait for the _____ of the _____ to help us was unacceptable as a solution?"

12. Describe the "one-two punch."

13. Why was debt important to Geneen?

14. What happens to a business that runs out of money?

15. The root to almost all problems is traced back to what?

16. How does one gain "comprehension of the numbers?"

17. Complete the following: "The truth is that the _____ of the numbers will make you free."

18. What does it mean to "read through the numbers?"

19. Why did ITT grow faster and with more success than other companies?

Chapter 10: Acquisitions and Growth

1. Why did ITT become a conglomerate?

2. Why did ITT increase its base of earnings in the United States?

3. When preparing for a discussion with the board about possible areas of expansion what was on the "one-sheet grid?"

4. Why did Geneen recommend financial services?

5. Why were pump companies a good concept?

6. What did Geneen learn about mundane businesses?

7. What was the rationale behind each company's business that Geneen looked for?

8. What did Geneen do with the management of the companies he acquired and what did he expect of the management that ran the companies acquired?

9. How many companies were ITT acquiring in 1968?

10. How did ITT pay for the companies they acquired?

11. When they found companies they liked, what did they pay for them?

12. Complete the following: "As the buyer, I had to be convinced that the future potential growth of that company made the price I was paying ____ for what I was getting."

13. What was meant by the previous quote?

14. Complete the following: "The road you ___ ____ can be as important in your life as the one you ___ _____."

15. What was Geneen's philosophy about conglomeration? Why was this counter to "Shoemaker, stick to your trade?"

16. Complete the following: "Actually, we have found that the growth in sales of a product in ____ _____ increases at a much faster rate than the decline in products _____ of favor."

17. Complete the following: "At ITT, each company _____ was responsible for everything that happened, good or bad, within his own _____ _____."

18. Why was Geneen successful as the leader of a conglomerate?

Chapter 11: Entrepreneurial Spirit

1. Complete the following: "By definition, an _____ is one who is in business for himself; he organizes, manages, and assumes the risks of a business enterprise."

2. Complete the following: "In truth, entrepreneurism is the _____ _____ of the philosophy of large publicly owned corporations."

3. How many brilliant moves does a bright man have to make to be considered on the fast track?

4. Are "big mistakes" the result of "big risks?"

5. Complete the following: "It is just that the more successful a company becomes, the more _____ __ it has to be to satisfy its conservative investors."

6. What do executives do when star salesmen earn more than they do?

7. How would you summarize Geneen's view of the Entrepreneur?

Chapter 12: The Board of Directors

Summarize the concepts you learn from this chapter.

Chapter 13: On Caring: A Summing Up

Summarize the concepts you learn from this chapter.

Appendix G: One Up on Wall Street [Part 1]

Purpose: To demonstrate the environmental factors that are required for a successful investor to analyze and select companies where the return is greater than the risk.

by Peter Lynch with John Rothchild
Questions from Reading Selected Chapters
(Each student will be prepared to discuss the answers to each of the following questions in class.)

Introduction to the Millennium Edition

1. Complete the following: "Never invest in any company before you've done the homework on the company's _____ _____, _____ _____, _____ _____, ____ _ _____ and so forth."

2. Complete the following: "If you own a retail company, another key factor in the analysis is figuring out whether the company is _____ __ ___ of its _____ ____."

3. To be a winning in the stock market what percent of your picks need to be winners?

4. Complete the following: "To help their shareholders avoid this double taxation, companies have abandoned the _____ in favor of the _____ strategy."

5. Complete the following: "It would be wonderful if we could ____ __ _____ with timely exits, but nobody has figured out how to _____ ___. Moreover, if you ____ stocks and ___ _ _____, how can you be certain you'll ___ ____ ____ ____ for the ____ _____?"

6. Why can't Europe respond to unemployment setbacks?

Introduction: The Advantages of Dumb Money

1. Complete the following: "Stop _____ __ _____."

2. Complete the following: "Dumb money is only _____ when it listens to the _____ _____."

3. What are the three good reasons to ignore what Peter Lynch is buying?

4. What is a Tenbagger?

5. Complete the following: "I stumbled onto big winners in _____ ____, the same way you could."

6. Complete the following: "Carolyn didn't need to be a textile analyst to realized that _____ __ _ _____ _____."

7. Summarize what was learned from the L'eggs experience.

8. Complete the following: "_____ _____ and _____ _____ is one of the critical elements of the analyst's job."

9. Complete the following: "People seem more comfortable investing in something about which they are entirely _____."

10. Complete the following: "if you couldn't tell if that was a _____ or a _____ ____ you should stay away from it."

11. If the first step is finding a promising company, what is the next step?

12. Lynch attributes his success at Magellan to what kind of stocks?

Chapter 1: The Making of a Stockpicker

1. Complete the following: "Ultimately it is not the _____ _____ nor even the _____ themselves that determine an investor's fate. It is the _____."

2. What is the Lynch Law?

3. What is the Peter Principle?

4. Complete the following: "it's difficult to predict _____, but also that small investors tend to be _____ and _____ precisely the wrong times, so it's _____-_____ to try to invest in good markets and get out of bad ones."

5. Complete the following: "In helping D. George Sullivan find his _____, I was helping myself find a _____."

6. Complete the following: "…studying _____ and _____ was much better preparation for the _____ _____ than, say, studying statistics. Investing in stocks is an ____, not a _____, and people who've been trained to rigidly _____ _____ have a big disadvantage."

7. Complete the following: "A lot of investors sit around and debate whether a stock is going up, as if the _____ _____ will give them the answer, instead of _____ __ _____."

8. What is the famous Newton quote Lynch states? How does this apply to this book?

9. Complete the following: "My distrust of _____ and _____ continues to this present day."

10. Complete the following: "The open-minded Ned Johnson watched me _____ __ _____ and _____ me on."

Chapter 2: The Wall Street Oxymorons

1. Complete the following: "it's increasingly likely that you're competing against _____ whenever you buy or sell shares. This is a lucky break for you."

2. Complete the following: "There are simply too many _____ between them [professionals] and the _____."

3. What is "Street Lag?"

4. Why do the fund managers avoid exciting stocks?

5. Complete the following: "The _____ the client, the more _____ the portfolio manager has to do to please him."

6. Complete the following: "It's exactly the kind of _____, _____, and _____ _____ company with an inscrutable name that I like to own."

7. What does Lynch mean by "burying the evidence?"

8. Complete the following: "…the stock market demands _____ as surely as it _____ the unconvinced."

Chapter 3: Is This Gambling, or What?

1. Was it a good deal for the Indians to sell Manhattan Island?

2. Why are long-term T-bonds a good deal?

3. Rank the performance of the following: Common stocks; Government bonds; Corporate bonds; and Treasury bills."

4. Why are common stocks a good investment?

5. Complete the following: "The point is that _____ change, there's no assurance that _____ _____ won't become minor, and there's no such thing as a can't miss _____ _____."

6. Complete the following: "Historically, stocks are embraced as _____ or dismissed as _____ in routine and circular fashion, and usually at the _____ times."

7. Complete the following: "…we can begin to separate gambling from investing not by the type of activity but by the _____, _____, and _____ of the participant."

8. What are three evidences that a company may be in a growth situation?

9. Complete the following: "Clearly the stock market has been a _____ worth taking---as long as you know how to _____ ___ _____."

Appendix H: One Up on Wall Street [Part 2]

Purpose: To show students how to investigate companies that show promise and what attributes they must demonstrate to be successful.

by Peter Lynch with John Rothchild
Questions from Reading Selected Chapters
(Each student will be prepared to discuss the answers to each of the following questions in class.)

Chapter 4: Passing the Mirror Test

1. Before anyone buys a stock they should address what three issues?

2. Complete the following: "It is no accident that people who are _____ in their houses are _____ in their stocks."

3. Complete the following: "'Never invest in anything that eats or needs repairs' may apply to _____, but its' malarkey when it comes to _____."

4. Complete the following: "Only invest what you could afford to lose without that loss having any effect on you daily _____ _____ in the foreseeable future."

5. What are the twelve qualities a stock investor should have?

6. How important in complete information?

7. Complete the following: "…by the time the _____ is received, the message may already have _____."

8. The unwary investor passes through what three emotional states?

9. Complete the following: "The true_____ waits for things to cool down and buys stocks that nobody cares about, and especially those that make _____ _____ _____."

Chapter 5: Is This a Good Market? Please Don't Ask

1. Complete the following: "You don't have to be able to _____ __ _____ _____ to make money in stocks."

2. Ed Hyman looks at what three indicators or economic movement?

3. Explain the Cocktail Theory.

4. Complete the following: "I don't believe in predicting the market. I believe in buying great companies---especially companies that are _____ and/or _____."

Chapter 6: Stalking the Tenbagger

1. Where are the three best places to look for a tenbagger?

2. How often does the average person come across a likely prospect in a year?

3. Complete the following: "So often we struggle to pick a _____ ____, when all the while a _____ ____ has been struggling to pick us."

4. What does Lynch mean by 'an edge?"

5. Complete the following: "Buyers and sellers of _____ _____ notice shortages and gluts, price changes and shifts in demand."

6. Grassroots observers can spot a turnaround how far in advance of the regular financial analyst?

7. What is the consumer's edge?

Chapter 7: I've Got It, I've Got It, What Is It?

1. Complete the following: "What you've got so far is simply __ _____ to a story that has to be developed."

2. How long does it take to develop the story?

3. What is the Charmin syndrome?

4. Complete the following: "What effect will the success of the product have on the _____ ___ _____."

5. How important is the size of the company?

6. What five things did a company that does everything right do?

7. What is the sure sign of a slow grower?

8. A stalwart generates what annual percent growth in earnings?

9. Fast growers are young companies that are overzealous and what else?

10. What are the most misunderstood of all the types of stocks?

11. What type of stocks result in unwary stock pickers being most easily parted from their money?

12. Complete the following: "Turnaround stocks make up lost ground ___ _____."

13. Complete the following: "...of all the categories of stocks, their ups and downs are ____ ____ to the general market."

14. What are the five various types of "Turnarounds?"

15. Define an "Asset Play" stock?

16. What is the single biggest quality an investor needs once they have found an asset play?

17. Complete the following: "Putting stocks in categories is the _____ ____ in developing the story."

Chapter 8: The Perfect Stock, What a Deal!

1. Does Lynch like simple situations?

2. Generally, the perfect stock will be in a company that could be run by ___ _____.

3. What does Lynch think of boring, dull or ridiculous?

4. What kind of name should the company have?

5. What about companies that do something disagreeable?

6. What does Lynch think of Spin-offs?

7. Is obscurity a factor in Lynch's perfect stock scenario?

8. What does the example of SCI suggest?

9. Complete the following: "There's no way to overstate the value of _____ _____ to a company or its shareholders."

10. Complete the following: "I always look for _____. The perfect company would have to have one."

11. Complete the following: "_____ _____ SUCH AS Robitussin or Tylenol, Coca-Cola or Marlboro, are almost as good as _____."

12. Complete the following: "Why take chances on fickle purchases when there's so much _____ business around?"

13. Complete the following: "…it's more significant when _____ at the _____ echelons add to their positions."

14. Complete the following: "…there's only one reason that _____ buy: They think the stock price is undervalued and will eventually ____ ____."

Appendix I: One Up on Wall Street [Part 3]

Purpose: To show students how attention to detail and looking at the right numbers can be rewarding for the successful investor.

by Peter Lynch with John Rothchild

Questions from Reading Selected Chapters

(Each student will be prepared to discuss the answers to each of the following questions in class.)

Chapter 9: Stocks I'd Avoid

1. Complete the following: "Hot stocks can go ___ _____, usually out of sight of any of the known landmarks of value, but since there's ____ __ _____ and thin air to support them, they fall just as quickly."

2. Complete the following: "In my experience the _____ ___ _____ almost never is---on Broadway."

3. What does diworseification mean?

4. Complete the following: "The trick is that you have to know how to make the _____ _____ and then manage them successfully."

5. What does "Synergy" mean in acquisitions?

6. Complete the following: "If a company must acquire something, I'd prefer it be __ _____ _____."

7. What is a "Whisper stock" and what does it lack?

8. Complete the following: "The company the sells 25 to 50 percent of its wares ot a _____ _____ is in a precarious situation."

Chapter 10: Earnings, Earnings, Earnings

1. Lynch says that what makes a company valuable and even more valuable in the future comes down to what two things?

2. How does Lynch define "Book Value" or "Net Economic Worth?"

3. Why is the capacity to earn income so important?

4. Which of the six categories of companies, as they relate to people, would you fall in?

5. What is a quick way to tell if a stock is overpriced?

6. What is the value of the P/E ratio?

7. Can P/E ratios be compared from industry to industry or over time?

8. Complete the following: "If you remember nothing else about p/e ratios, remember to avoid stocks with _____ _____ _____."

9. Complete the following: "…when you find that a few stocks are selling at inflated prices relative to earnings, it's likely that _____ _____ are selling at inflated prices relative to earnings."

10. Complete the following: "Interest rates have a large effect on the _____ ____ _____, since investors pay more for stocks when interest rates are low and bonds are less attractive."

11. What are the five basic ways a company can increase earnings?

Chapter 11: The Two-Minute Drill

1. Complete the following: "The next step is to learn as much as possible about what the company is doing to bring about the _____ _____, ____ _____ _____, or whatever happy event is expected to occur."

2. Complete the following: "…something has to happen to keep the _____ ____ ____. The more certain you are about what that something is, the better you'll be able to follow the script."

3. What things do you look for in each category of stock?

4. Why was La Quinta a great stock?

5. Complete the following: "I always try to learn something new from every investment _____ I have."

6. Complete the following: "I followed up on this conversation by spending ____ ____ in _____ _____ La Quintas while I was on the road talking to other companies."

7. Complete the following: "From the prospectus of the stock offering, I learned that the company was not going to burden itself with _____ ____ _____.'

8. What did Lynch learn from Bildner's?

Chapter 12: Getting the Facts

1. Complete the following: "Chairmen, presidents, vice presidents, and analysts fill me in on _____ _____, _____ ____, _____-_____ _____, and anything else that's relevant to future results."

2. What is the old "Oracle Rule?"

3. What four things do you want the firm's analysts to provide, once they realize that you're serious?

4. What were the seven rapid fire questions that Lynch asked about La Quinta?

5. What did Mark Twain say about speculating in stocks?

6. What does "held in street name" mean?

7. What does Lynch look for when visiting the headquarters of a company?

8. What is the value of attending the company's annual meeting?

9. Complete the following: "I could never prove this scientifically, but if you can't imagine how a company respresentative could ever _____ ___ _____, chances are you're right."

10. What is the value of wandering through stores and tasting things?

11. What is the value of questioning customers who have purchased the product?

12. What is a couple of sure signs of prosperity for a company?

13. What do you really want to know in the short exercise of getting the facts?

Chapter 13: Some Famous Numbers

1. Complete the following: "...the first thing I want to know is what that product means to the company in question. What _____ ___ _____ does it represent?"

2. Complete the following: "The p/e ratio of any company that's fairly priced will equal its _____ ____ [of earnings]."

3. What are the general rules for very positive and very negative PEG ratios?

4. Why is the cash position important?

5. Complete the following: "How much does the company _____, and how much does it _____?"

6. What is the normal percent of equity and debt on a company balance sheet?

7. What determines if a company will survive or go bankrupt in a crisis?

8. What is the "Bladder Theory" of corporate finance?

9. Complete the following: "Then again, the small companies that don't pay dividends are likely to _____ much faster because of it."

10. What relationship does the book value have to the actual worth of a company?

11. Are foreign companies a good bet?

12. What is the difference between cash flow and free cash flow?

13. What do you check for relative to inventories?

14. Complete the following: "If you find a business that can get away with _____ _____ year after year without losing customers, you've got a terrific investment."

15. What is the difference between a 10 % grower and a 20% grower?

16. Complete the following: "What you want, then, is a relatively high _____-_____ in a long term stock that you plan to hold through good times and bad, and a relatively low _____-_____ in a successful turnaround."

Chapter 14: Rechecking the Story

What are the three phases of expansion?

Chapter 15: The Final Checklist

What is the value of the phrase: "The more you know the better?"

Appendix J: LTCM

1998
Collapse of Long Term Capital Management (LTCM)

LTCM, founded by the former head of Salomon Brothers John Meriwether in 1994 is a hedge fund that traded derivatives such as options and swaps using very complex mathematical models. The hedge fund employed two Nobel Prize winning economists Myron Scholes and Robert C. Merton. The fund had an initial capital of $1 billion pooled from interested investors. At the heart of its trading system lies a very complicated mathematical model for pricing options. This system, formulated by Scholes and Merton is supposed to take irrational human emotions away and introduce a systematic way of trading that will maximize profits based on historical statistics on the market. In other words, risk management is decided by their proprietary trading system based on quantitative analysis. Large investment banks and big name investors invested a total of $1.3 billion and LTCM's first few operating years were very fruitful proving that mathematics takes away the risk generated by traditional methods of investing. In 1998, Long Term Capital Management raised the stakes confident that their quantitative methods should limit loses and borrowed $125 billion with only $5 billion in assets, this is big time leveraging.

LTCM specialized in selling call and put options that based on their quantitative methods would not be exercised. In other words, their system relies on steady and stable markets so that the strike prices of the options they sold would not be exercised. LTCM ignored the fact that option prices were so high indicating an imminent volatile market, but their complex math based trading box says otherwise, so they went ahead with the plan.

That same year in August 17 1998, Russia became a casualty of the Asian financial meltdown and suffered their own financial crisis; as a result, Russia was forced to devalue their currency, the Ruble. The volatility that LTCM thought was improbable was unfolding globally as Japanese and European bonds was under a major selling frenzy for the safety of US treasury bonds. The resulting volatility on the bond markets spilled through the equities markets and stock prices were wildly swinging in all directions. The options that LTCM thought would never be exercised were exercised as volatility in the stock market reached the strike prices of the options they sold. By August of 1998, Long Term Capital Management was bleeding in capital as it lost over $1.85 billion. As LTCM tried to contain loses by exiting most of their positions, this further triggered fear in the markets and volatility continued. The Federal Reserve took notice of this event and bailed out the hedge fund with $1 billion in four months. The efforts by the Federal Reserve did not stop the LTCM from losing a total of $4.6 billion. How can a group of intelligent people who formulated a mathematically sophisticated trading system fail to see this event from possibly happening? One factor is that the data contained in their formulas only goes back 5 years' worth of historical figures. But the ultimate answer may lie on the fact that markets are not ran by numbers, behind the curtain of this seemingly complex trading arena is a group of people which are susceptible to irrationality. What LTCM failed to see is that human behavior cannot be translated into numbers.[37]

VIDEOS:
http://prezi.com/k3i6ssnuc36f/the-fall-of-ltcm/

---

http://www.youtube.com/watch?v=dsrOXJwGwtk

http://www.youtube.com/watch?v=Jzl39jqZjsw

http://www.youtube.com/watch?v=436cfNtDp3A&list=PL7A5F7566C97D0F0D

http://www.youtube.com/watch?v=rEFTHbG5JuI

http://www.youtube.com/watch?v=G17rx7H3DtI

---

[37] http://history.econtrader.com/collapse_of_ltcm.htm

Appendix K: Dot-com Bubble

2000
Dot-com bubble

Internet technology started to pick up its pace during the mid 90's. Although the technology at its earliest form existed since 1958 in the form of ARPA (Advanced Research Projects Agency), it is not until the last quarter of the 90's did the internet become practical enough for commercial use. The concept of a global network spurred new business models based entirely on the internet taking advantage of network effects. This effect is supposed to be an efficient means to spread consumer awareness resulting in huge potential profits. In the mid 90's low interest rates in the United States freed up more investment capital through lending. Most of the available capital was channeled into new internet companies with business plans to monopolize their respective sector. However, every new internet company has the same business plan and most of them were clearly devoid of a plan to be efficiently profitable. Venture capitalists simply funded companies anticipating the enormous potential of the internet. In order to get funded, companies only have to put a .com suffix on their name ignoring their balance sheet as there really is nothing to see there. Internet companies going public such as the globe.com saw their stock jump up to over 606% on the first trading day. Investors totally turned irrational at the height of this mania that companies such as webvan.com also got fresh supply of funds even if its business model, an online grocery is severely flawed like a very low profit margin and the fact that their fleets of delivery trucks are extremely sensitive to the price of crude oil.

Looking beyond the mania generated by the internet bubble, investors are right in a way. The internet has become a global market force with users reaching almost a quarter of the earth's population. The only thing is, the current dominating state of the internet happened 10 years after the burst of the dot-com bubble. The idea of the internet being a global market force was cashed in too early. Everybody tried to get in to the boom believing that they might get left out once the price has reached a higher plateau. Investors simply overvalued internet companies during the late 90s because the traditional pricing of companies based on its earnings are replaced by the speed on which a company would grow. The capital received by internet companies that failed simply used it for advertisements so that the public would become aware of their presence. The Federal Reserve is aware of this new developing mania and as of 1999, it slowly raised interest rates to slow down the flow of capital. Since internet companies do not have a positive cash flow from their operations, they rely on funding and profits from new share issues. When capital becomes tight as a result of expensive lending rates, dot-com companies are left without cash to burn. The idea of growth over profits failed most of these internet companies when funding is no longer easy to acquire. By March of 2000 the technology heavy NASDAQ fell from its peak of 5132.52 to 3,649 in April. People realized the over valuation of these profitless dot-com companies when capital dried up as a result of higher interest rates and brought insanity back into the market. However, most internet companies with sound business models survived the crash no matter how heavy their stocks got hit like Yahoo and Amazon. The then profitless Google stayed on the sidelines at the height of the bubble and only began offering shares to the public four years later on August 19, 2004.[38]

VIDEOS:
http://www.youtube.com/watch?v=W2FybpdrlYM

http://www.youtube.com/watch?v=0E2ufujhYNI

http://www.youtube.com/watch?v=3K-QX8g5fTI

[38] http://history.econtrader.com/dot_com_bubble.htm

Appendix L: Housing Bubble

2007
U.S Housing Market bubble and crash

After years of quantitative easing and loose government regulation, the U.S Housing market finally revealed that it turned into a bubble and finally collapsed. Houses are assets that are considered hard to liquidate compared to other assets such as stocks and yet real estate was traded not because people need roofs on top of their heads but simply by pure speculation. The housing markets have been far less volatile than that of the stock market in fact, house prices remained at a steady upward direction since the end of WW2 but not until it started go out of control in the 2000s. The world has actually forgotten the lessons learned from numerous bubbles that occured throught history. The most recent one similar to the housing market bubble is the Japanese asset price bubble in the 1980s where house prices shot up to the point that it became too expensive for the average Japanese citizen to afford.

The combination of declining interest rates and government pressure to lenders, made the housing market at first a very affordable venture. The Bush administration further pushed this in 2003 with the American Dream Downpayment Act this subsidized first time homebuyers and asked lenders to ease the pressure on subprime borrowers to provide full personal and financial documentation to obtain a loan. Fanny Mae and Freddie Mac were also put under pressure to open its loan vaults to subprime clients through a government guarantee of the loans. With all the systems in place, this jump started the housing market speculation where the ease of obtaining a loan supplied the needed demand for real estate brokers to finally raise prices in increments, slowly. As house prices went up, the Federal Reserve's concern of rampant inflation caused by this free floating money from easy loans prompted them to slowly tighten interest rates. Most subprime borrowers are on variable interest rate loans which means, it is very affordable if the interest rate is low but as the Fed slowly increased rates to control inflation, their monthly payments also increased to the point that they could no longer afford to pay the mortgage and still have something left for their other basic expenses. House prices in 2006 at its peak has gone up to ridiculously high levels that most lenders are not willing to make loans. The extremely high house prices and the lack of available money from lenders drastically reduced demand for new houses and, combined with the defaulting subprime borrowers, the balance sheets of numerous subprime lenders were permanently damaged.

Some events that lead into the confirmation of the crash started with Freddie Mac's announcement that it would no longer purchase risky subprime loans followed by the subprime lender New Century Financial's bankruptcy. By August of 2007, subprime loans are extinct, finding one is mostly a fantasy American Home Mortgage also filed for bankruptcy.[39]

---

[39] http://history.econtrader.com/us_housing_market_bubble.htm

Appendix M: Other Stuff
Accountants Work Tonight (The Lion Sleep Tonight)

Intro: Weeheeheehee dee heeheeheehee weeoh aweem away
Weeheeheehee dee heeheeheehee weeoh aweem away

Chorus:
(A-low a-leh, a-low a-leh, a-low a-leh, a-low a-leh,)
(A-low a-leh, a-low a-leh, a-low a-leh, a-low a-leh,)

In the office, the busy office
Accountants work tonight
In the office, the busy office
Accountants, work tonight

Intro and Chorus

Post transactions and organize them,
Accountants work tonight.
Post transactions and organize them,
Accountants work tonight.

Intro and Chorus

Balance Sheet, Cash and Income Statements,
Accountants work tonight.
Balance Sheet, Cash and Income Statements
Accountants work tonight.

Intro, Chorus and Intro

A-low a-leh stand for A L OE (Assets, Liabilities and Owner's Equity)

R.O.I.C. (YMCA)

Hey boss there's no need to feel down
I said hey boss pick yourself off the ground
I said hey boss find out if you are sound
There's no need to be unhappy

Hey boss there's a place you can go
I said Hey boss when you really want to know
At Business Allstars I'm sure you will find
Analysis of every kind.

It's fun to calculate the R.O.I.C.
It's fun to calculate the R.O.I.C.
They have everything for a boss to enjoy.
And lots of tools you can employ.

It's fun to calculate the R.O.I.C.
It's fun to calculate the R.O.I.C.
Is your company clean?
Is the bottom-line real
Let me tell you it's a big deal.

R.O.I.C.
calculate the R.O.I.C.
Hey boss, hey boss, there is no time to lose,
Hey boss, hey boss, it's your time to choose

R.O.I.C.
R.O.I.C.
R.O.I.C.
R.O.I.C.

Cash Flow (Dry Bones)

Ezekiel cried, "Free Cash Flow!"
Ezekiel cried, "Free Cash Flow!"
Ezekiel cried, "Free Cash Flow!"
"Oh, hear the word of the Lord."

The gross sales connected to the expense,
The expense connected to the ebit,
The ebit connected to the tax rate,
The tax rate connected to the nopat,
The nopat connected to the cap change,
The cap change connected to the cash flow,
Oh, hear the word of the Lord!

Cash flow, cash flow gonna walk aroun',
Cash flow, cash flow gonna walk aroun',
Cash flow, cash flow gonna walk aroun',
Oh, hear the word of the Lord.

The cash flow connected to the cap change,
The cap change connected to the nopat,
The nopat connected to the tax rate,
The tax rate connected to the ebit,
The ebit connected to the expense,
The expense connected to the gross sales,
Oh, hear the word of the Lord!

Weighted Average (Love Me Tender)

Weighted Average
cost of cap,
Let me now extol
All the virtues you possess
In your finance roll.

Weighted Average
cost of cap,
All my dreams fulfill.
You provide the discount rate
and you always will.

Weighted Average
cost of cap,
Treat me oh so dear.
You're the measure I must beat,
The hurdle rate to clear.

Weighted Average
cost of cap,
Tell me you are mine.
Cost of equity and debt,
Till the end of time.

(When at last my dreams come true
and I see you there
Happiness applying you
everything must bare).

Stock Value (White Christmas)

I'm dreaming of a stock value
just like the one I used to know.
Where the markets glisten
Investors listen
To hear we had great cash flow.

I'm dreaming of a stock value
That every analyst will love.
May residual value be bright
And our EVA go out of sight.

I'm dreaming of a stock value
just like the one I used to know.
Where the markets glisten
Investors listen
To hear we had great cash flow.

I'm dreaming of a stock value
That every analyst will love.
May residual value be bright
And our EVA go out of sight.

Moody's (Venus)

Hey Moody's, Oh Moody's

Moody's if you will
Please give a corporate rating with your skill
A rating that will signal everyone
It's correctly done by you.

Moody's make it fair
We love it when the interest rate we bare
Is based upon the data you have found
And says that we are sound and good

Moody's masters of rates that you are
Surely the things we ask
Can't be too great a task

Moody's if you do
We promise that we always will be true
And get us all the credit that we need
As long as we both succeed

Moody's masters of rates that you are
Surely the things we ask
Can't be too great a task

Moody's if you do
We promise that we always will be true
And get us all the credit that we need
As long as we both succeed

Hey Moody's Oh Moody's
Make our rates come down

Compare (Michelle)

Chorus:
Compar-i-son,
Based upon the data that we share
Do compare.

chorus

We're better, we're better, we're better.
That's all we want to say.
Until we find a way
we'll share financials and we know that
you'll understand.

chorus

We need to, we need to, we need to.
We need to make you see,
Improving constantly
Until we do we're hoping you will
Know what we mean.

We want to, we want to, we want to
make changes that we know
will soon begin to show
until we do we're telling you so
you'll understand.

chorus